The Kaggle Workbook

Self-learning exercises and valuable insights for Kaggle data science competitions

Konrad Banachewicz

Luca Massaron

BIRMINGHAM—MUMBAI

Packt and this book are not officially connected with Kaggle. This book is an effort from the Kaggle community of experts to help more developers.

The Kaggle Workbook

Lead Senior Publishing Product Manager: Tushar Gupta

Acquisition Editor – Peer Reviews: Gaurav Gavas

Project Editor: Parvathy Nair

Content Development Editor: Bhavesh Amin

Copy Editor: Safis Editing

Technical Editor: Karan Sonawane

Proofreader: Safis Editing

Indexer: Pratik Shirodkar

Presentation Designer: Rajesh Shirsath

Developer Relations Marketing Executive: Monika Sangwan

First published: February 2023

Production reference: 2200223

Published by Packt Publishing Ltd.
Livery Place
35 Livery Street
Birmingham
B3 2PB, UK.

ISBN 978-1-80461-121-0

www.packt.com

Contributors

About the authors

Konrad Banachewicz is a data science manager with experience that goes back more than he would care to mention. He holds a PhD in statistics from Vrije Universiteit Amsterdam, where he focused on problems of extreme dependency modeling in credit risk. He slowly moved from classic statistics toward machine learning and into the business applications world.

Konrad worked in a variety of financial institutions on an array of data problems and visited all stages of the data product cycle, from translating business requirements ("what do they really need"); through data acquisition ("spreadsheets and flat files? Really?"), wrangling, modeling, and testing (the actual fun part), all the way to presenting the results to people allergic to mathematical terminology (which is the majority of business). He has visited different ends of the frequency spectrum in finance (from high-frequency trading to credit risk, and everything in between), predicted potato prices, analyzed anomalies in industrial equipment, and optimized recommendations. He is a staff data scientist at Adevinta.

As a person who himself stood on the shoulders of giants, Konrad believes in sharing knowledge with others: it is very important to know how to approach practical problems with data science methods, but also how not to do it.

Luca Massaron is a data scientist with more than a decade of experience in transforming data into smarter artifacts, solving real-world problems, and generating value for businesses and stakeholders. He is the author of best-selling books on AI, machine learning, and algorithms. Luca is also a Kaggle Grandmaster, who reached number 7 in the worldwide user rankings for his performance in data science competitions, and a **Google Developer Expert (GDE)** in machine learning.

My warmest thanks go to my family, Yukiko and Amelia, for their support and loving patience as I prepared this new book in a long series.

About the reviewers

Laura Fink works as a senior data scientist for H2O.ai, and her main interest is in building AI tools for unstructured data. Within the field of machine learning, she is especially interested in deep learning and unsupervised methods.

Before joining H2O.ai, she was the Head of Data Science at the software development company Micromata, building a data science team to open up new business opportunities. Her mission has always been to help customers to make data-driven decisions by using data science and machine learning to solve business problems.

Laura holds a master's degree in physics from the Ludwig Maximilian University of Munich with a focus on biophysics and nonlinear dynamical systems. She had her first contact with machine learning during her master's thesis in 2015 and has been fascinated by its potential ever since. After joining Kaggle in the same year, she was immediately hooked by the platform and its awesome community. As a Notebooks Grandmaster, she enjoys sharing her insights and learning experiences with the community by writing tutorials and detailed exploratory analyses.

Gabriel Preda is a principal data scientist at Endava. He worked for more than 20 years in software engineering, holding both development and management positions. He is passionate about data science and machine learning and is constantly contributing to Kaggle, being currently a triple Kaggle Grandmaster.

Pietro Marinelli has consistently been ranked among the top data scientists in the world on the Google AI platform, Kaggle. He has reached 3rd position among Italian data scientists and 141st among 150,000 data scientists around the world. Due to his work on Kaggle, he has been honored to participate as a speaker at Paris Kaggle Day, January 2019.

He has been working with artificial intelligence, text analytics, and many other data science techniques for many years, and has more than 15 years of experience in designing products based on data for different industries. He has produced a variety of algorithms, ranging from predictive modeling to advanced simulation, to support top management's business decisions for a variety of multinational companies. He is currently collaborating as a reviewer for Packt, reviewing AI books.

Due to his achievements in the AI field in February 2020, he has been honored to participate as a speaker at the Italian Chamber of Deputies to talk about the role of AI in the new global landscape.

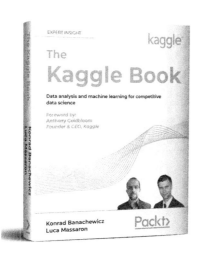

Book aims:
Structured learning on the techniques to succeed in Kaggle competitions and data science projects

Topics include:
Data, metrics, validation, optimization, machine learning, and creating data science portfolios

Learn the fundamentals

‹packt›

Move up the leaderboard

Book aims:
Practical walkthroughs of a selection of competitions to show you how to create effective solutions

Topics include:
Time series, vision transformers, natural language processing, gradient boosting, and autoencoders

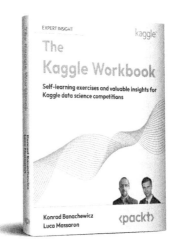

Join our book's Discord space

Join our Discord community to meet like-minded people and learn alongside more than 2000 members at:

https://packt.link/KaggleDiscord

Table of Contents

Preface

When we started planning *The Kaggle Book*, we had more than 85,117 novices (as they have at least just registered) and 57,426 contributors (as they have at least filled their profile) present at the time on the Kaggle platform. We wondered how to help them break the ice with data science competitions on Kaggle. We then decided to provide them with the best available information about Kaggle and data science competitions and help them to start their journey in the best possible way, thanks to hints and suggestions by over 30 Kaggle Masters and Grandmasters.

Only when we had completed our work, we realized that there was little space left in the book for anything else and that, regrettably, we had to exclude some practical demonstrations and examples. However, practice sometimes is as important as theory (we know about it very well since we are applied data scientists!), and theory cannot be considered complete without any practice. Finally, *The Kaggle Workbook* is here to supplement *The Kaggle Book* by providing you with guided exercises to put some of the ideas found in *The Kaggle Book* into practice.

Strictly speaking, in this workbook, you will find:

- The exploration of an emblematic selection of competitions (tabular, forecasting, computer vision, and natural language processing) where we demonstrate how a simple and effective solution can be derived for each of them.
- Reference to concepts and ideas to be found in the original Kaggle Book.
- Some challenges for the readers, as we pose some questions (and exercises) help hone your skills on the same proposed competitions or in analogous ones.

First, by reading *The Kaggle Book* and then practicing on *The Kaggle Workbook*, you'll have all the skills, both theory-based and hands-on, necessary to compete on Kaggle for glory, fun, or learning, and gathering interesting, applied projects to present in a job interview, or for your own portfolio!

Let's not wait; let's start practicing now!

Who this book is for

This book has been written for all the readers of *The Kaggle Book* and for all the Kaggle novices and contributors who want practical experience in past competitions to reinforce their learning before delving into competitions on Kaggle.

What this book covers

Chapter 1, The Most Renowned Tabular Competition – Porto Seguro's Safe Driver Prediction. In this competition, you are asked to solve a common problem in insurance to figure out who is going to have an auto insurance claim in the next year. We guide you in properly using LightGBM, denoising autoencoders, and how to effectively blend them.

Chapter 2, The Makridakis Competitions – M5 on Kaggle for Accuracy and Uncertainty. In this competition based on Walmart's daily sales time series of items hierarchically arranged into departments, categories, and stores spread across three U.S. states, we recreate the 4th-place solution's ideas from Monsaraida to demonstrate how we can effectively use LightGBM for this time series problem.

Chapter 3, Vision Competition – Cassava Leaf Disease Classification. In this contest, the participants were tasked with classifying crowdsourced photos of cassava plants grown by farmers in Uganda. We use the multiclass problem to demonstrate how to build a complete pipeline for image classification and show how this baseline can be utilized to construct a competitive solution using a vast array of possible extensions.

Chapter 4, NLP Competition – Google Quest Q&A Labeling, discusses a contest focused on predicting human responders' evaluations of subjective aspects of a question-answer pair, where an understanding of context was crucial. Casting the challenge as a multiclass classification problem, we build a baseline solution exploring the semantic characteristics of a corpus, followed by an examination of more advanced methods that were necessary for leaderboard ascent.

To get the most out of this book

The Python code proposed in this book has been designed to run on a Kaggle Notebook without any installation on a local computer. Therefore, don't worry about what machine you have available and about what version of Python package you have to install. All you need is a computer with access to the internet and a free Kaggle account. (you will find instructions about the procedures in *Chapter 3* of *The Kaggle Book*). If you don't have a free Kaggle account yet, just go to www.kaggle.com and follow the instructions on the website.

When referred to a link, just explore it: you can find code available on public Kaggle Notebooks that you can reuse or further materials to illustrate concepts and ideas that we outlined in the book.

Download the example code files

The code bundle for the book is hosted on GitHub at `https://github.com/PacktPublishing/The-Kaggle-Workbook`. We also have other code bundles from our rich catalog of books and videos available at `https://github.com/PacktPublishing/`. Check them out!

Download the color images

We also provide a PDF file that has color images of the screenshots/diagrams used in this book. You can download it here: `https://packt.link/Rgb6B`.

Conventions used

There are a few text conventions used throughout this book.

`CodeInText`: Indicates code words in text, database table names, folder names, filenames, file extensions, pathnames, dummy URLs, user input, and Twitter handles. For example, "An important component of our feature extraction pipeline is the `TfidfVectorizer`."

A block of code is set as follows:

```
!pip install transformers
import transformer
```

Any command-line input or output is written as follows:

```
LightGBM CV Gini Normalized Score: 0.289 (0.015)
```

Bold: Indicates a new term, an important word, or words that you see on the screen, for example, in menus or dialog boxes, also appear in the text like this. For example: " We will evaluate the performance of our baseline model using **Out-Of-Fold** (**OOF**) cross validation."

`Link`: Indicates a hyperlink to a web page containing additional information on a topic or to a resource on Kaggle.

Exercises are displayed as follows:

<hr>

Exercise Number

Exercise Notes (write down any notes or workings that will help you):

Warnings or important notes appear like this.

 Tips and tricks appear like this.

Get in touch

Feedback from our readers is always welcome.

General feedback: Email feedback@packtpub.com and mention the book's title in the subject of your message. If you have questions about any aspect of this book, please email us at questions@packtpub.com.

Errata: Although we have taken every care to ensure the accuracy of our content, mistakes do happen. If you have found a mistake in this book, we would be grateful if you could report this to us. Please visit http://www.packtpub.com/submit-errata, select your book, click on the **Submit Errata** link, and enter the details.

Piracy: If you come across any illegal copies of our works in any form on the internet, we would be grateful if you would provide us with the location address or website name. Please contact us at copyright@packtpub.com with a link to the material.

If you are interested in becoming an author: If there is a topic that you have expertise in, and you are interested in either writing or contributing to a book, please visit http://authors.packtpub.com.

Share your thoughts

Once you've read *The Kaggle Workbook*, we'd love to hear your thoughts! Scan the QR code below to go straight to the Amazon review page for this book and share your feedback.

https://packt.link/r/1-804-61121-2

Your review is important to us and the tech community and will help us make sure we're delivering excellent quality content.

Download a free PDF copy of this book

Thanks for purchasing this book!

Do you like to read on the go but are unable to carry your print books everywhere? Is your eBook purchase not compatible with the device of your choice?

Don't worry, now with every Packt book you get a DRM-free PDF version of that book at no cost.

Read anywhere, any place, on any device. Search, copy, and paste code from your favorite technical books directly into your application.

The perks don't stop there, you can get exclusive access to discounts, newsletters, and great free content in your inbox daily

Follow these simple steps to get the benefits:

1. Scan the QR code or visit the link below

https://packt.link/free-ebook/9781804611210

2. Submit your proof of purchase
3. That's it! We'll send your free PDF and other benefits to your email directly

1

The Most Renowned Tabular Competition – Porto Seguro's Safe Driver Prediction

Learning how to reach the top on the leaderboard in any Kaggle competition requires patience, diligence, and many attempts to learn the best way to compete and achieve top results. For this reason, we have thought of a workbook that can help you build those skills faster by trying some Kaggle competitions of the past and learning how to reach the top of the leaderboard by reading discussions, reusing notebooks, engineering features, and training various models.

We start with one of the most renowned tabular competitions, Porto Seguro's Safe Driver Prediction. In this competition, you are asked to solve a common problem in insurance and figure out who is going to have a car insurance claim in the next year. Such information is useful to increase the insurance fee for drivers more likely to have a claim and to lower it for those less likely to.

In illustrating the key insights and technicalities necessary for cracking this competition, we will show you the necessary code and ask you to study topics and answer questions found in *The Kaggle Book* itself. Therefore, without much more ado, let's start this new learning path of yours.

In this chapter, you will learn:

- How to tune and train a LightGBM model
- How to build a denoising autoencoder and how to use it to feed a neural network
- How to effectively blend models that are quite different from each other

All the code files for this chapter can be found at Change to `https://packt.link/kwbchp1`

Understanding the competition and the data

Porto Seguro is the third largest insurance company in Brazil (it operates in Brazil and Uruguay), offering car insurance coverage as well as many other insurance products, having used analytical methods and machine learning for the past 20 years to tailor their prices and make auto insurance coverage more accessible to more drivers. To explore new ways to achieve their task, they sponsored a competition (`https://www.kaggle.com/competitions/porto-seguro-safe-driver-prediction`), expecting Kagglers to come up with new and better methods of solving some of their core analytical problems.

The competition is aimed at having Kagglers build a model that predicts the probability that a driver will initiate an auto insurance claim in the next year, which is a quite common kind of task (the sponsor mentions it as a "classical challenge for insurance"). This kind of information about the probability of filing a claim can be quite precious for an insurance company. Without such a model, insurance companies may only charge a flat premium to customers irrespective of their risk, or, if they have a poorly performing model, they may charge a mismatched premium to them. Inaccuracies in profiling the customers' risk can therefore result in charging a higher insurance cost to good drivers and reducing the price for the bad ones. The impact on the company would be two-fold: good drivers will look elsewhere for their insurance and the company's portfolio will be overweighed with bad ones (technically, the company would have a bad loss ratio: `https://www.investopedia.com/terms/l/loss-ratio.asp`). Instead, if the company can correctly estimate the claim likelihood, they can ask for a fair price from their customers, thus increasing their market share, having more satisfied customers and a more balanced customer portfolio (better loss ratio), and managing their reserves better (the money the company sets aside for paying claims).

To do so, the sponsor provided training and test datasets, and the competition was ideal for anyone since the dataset was not very large and was very well prepared.

As stated on the page of the competition devoted to presenting the data (`https://www.kaggle.com/competitions/porto-seguro-safe-driver-prediction/data`):

Features that belong to similar groupings are tagged as such in the feature names (e.g., ind, reg, car, calc).

> *In addition, feature names include the postfix bin to indicate binary features and cat to indicate categorical features. Features without these designations are either continuous or ordinal. Values of -1 indicate that the feature was missing from the observation. The target column signifies whether or not a claim was filed for that policy holder.*

The data preparation for the competition was carefully conducted to avoid any leak of information, and although secrecy has been maintained about the meaning of the features, it is quite clear that the different used tags refer to specific kinds of features commonly used in motor insurance modeling:

- ind refers to "individual characteristics"
- car refers to "car characteristics"
- calc refers to "calculated features"
- reg refers to "regional/geographic features"

As for the individual features, there was much speculation about their meaning during the competition. See for instance:

- https://www.kaggle.com/competitions/porto-seguro-safe-driver-prediction/discussion/41489, where Raddar suggests that the feature ps_car_13 could represent the distance driven between bi-yearly mandatory car checkups.
- https://www.kaggle.com/competitions/porto-seguro-safe-driver-prediction/discussion/41488, where Raddar suggests that the feature ps_car_12 instead represents engine car cylinder capacity.
- https://www.kaggle.com/competitions/porto-seguro-safe-driver-prediction/discussion/41057, where you can read about the suggestion to attribute some feature as derived from Porto Seguro's online quote form.

In spite of all these and more efforts, in the end the meaning of most of the features has remained a mystery up until now.

The interesting facts about this competition are that:

1. The data is real-world, though the features are anonymous.
2. The data is very well prepared, without leakages of any sort (no magic features here – a magic feature is a feature that by skillful processing can provide high predictive power to your models in a Kaggle competition).
3. The test dataset not only holds the same categorical levels as the training dataset; it also seems to be from the same distribution, although Yuya Yamamoto argues that preprocessing the data with t-SNE leads to a failing adversarial validation test (https://www.kaggle.com/competitions/porto-seguro-safe-driver-prediction/discussion/44784).

Exercise 1

As a first exercise, referring to the contents and the code in *The Kaggle Book* related to adversarial validation (starting from page 179), prove that the training and test data most probably originated from the same data distribution.

Exercise Notes (write down any notes or workings that will help you):

An interesting post by Tilii (Mensur Dlakic, Associate Professor at Montana State University: `https://www.kaggle.com/competitions/porto-seguro-safe-driver-prediction/discussion/42197`) demonstrates using t-SNE that "there are many people who are very similar in terms of their insurance parameters, yet some of them will file a claim and others will not." What Tilii mentions is quite typical of what happens in insurance, where for certain priors (insurance parameters) there is the same probability of something happening, but that event will happen or not based on how long we observe the sequence of events.

Take, for instance, IoT and telematic data in insurance. It is quite common to analyze a driver's behavior to predict if they will file a claim in the future. If your observation period is too short (for instance, one year, as in the case of this competition), it may happen that even very bad drivers won't have a claim because there is a low probability that such an event will occur in a short period of time, even for a bad driver. Similar ideas are discussed by Andy Harless (`https://www.kaggle.com/competitions/porto-seguro-safe-driver-prediction/discussion/42735`), who argues instead that the real task of the competition is to guess *"the value of a latent continuous variable that determines which drivers are more likely to have accidents"* because actually *"making a claim is not a characteristic of a driver; it's a result of chance."*

Understanding the evaluation metric

The metric used in the competition is the **normalized Gini coefficient** (named after the similar Gini coefficient/index used in economics), which has been previously used in another competition, the Allstate Claim Prediction Challenge (`https://www.kaggle.com/competitions/ClaimPredictionChallenge`). From that competition, we can get a very clear explanation of what this metric is about:

> *When you submit an entry, the observations are sorted from "largest prediction" to "smallest prediction." This is the only step where your predictions come into play, so only the order determined by your predictions matters. Visualize the observations arranged from left to right, with the largest predictions on the left. We then move from left to right, asking "In the leftmost x% of the data, how much of the actual observed loss have you accumulated?" With no model, you can expect to accumulate 10% of the loss in 10% of the predictions, so no model (or a "null" model) achieves a straight line. We call the area between your curve and this straight line the Gini coefficient.*

> *There is a maximum achievable area for a "perfect" model. We will use the normalized Gini coefficient by dividing the Gini coefficient of your model by the Gini coefficient of the perfect model.*

There is no formulation proposed by the organizers of the competition for the Normalized Gini apart from this verbose description, but by reading the notebook from Mohsin Hasan (`https://www.kaggle.com/code/tezdhar/faster-gini-calculation/notebook`), we can figure out that it is calculated in two steps and can obtain some easy to understand pseudocode that reveals its inner workings. First, you get the Gini coefficient for your predictions, then you normalize it by dividing it by another Gini coefficient computed by pretending you have perfect predictions. Here is the pseudocode for the Gini coefficient:

order = indexes of sorted predictions (expressed as probabilities from lowest to highest)

sorted_actual = actual[order] = ground truth values sorted based on indexes of sorted predictions

cumsum_sorted_actual = cumulated sum of the sorted ground truth values

n = number of predictions

gini_coef = (sum(cumsum_sorted_actual) / sum(sorted_actual) - (n + 1) / 2) / n

Once you have the Gini coefficient for your predictions, you need to divide it by the Gini coefficient you compute using the ground truth values as they were your predictions (the case of having perfect predictions)

norm_gini_coef = gini_coef(predictions) / gini_coef(ground truth)

Another good explanation is provided in the notebook by Kilian Batzner: `https://www.kaggle.com/code/batzner/gini-coefficient-an-intuitive-explanation`. Using clear plots and some toy examples, Kilian tries to make sense of a not-so-common metric, yet routinely used by the actuarial departments of insurance companies.

The metric can be approximated by the ROC-AUC score or the Mann–Whitney U non-parametric statistical test (since the U statistic is equivalent to the area under the receiver operating characteristic curve – AUC) because it approximately corresponds to 2 * ROC-AUC - 1. Hence, maximizing the ROC-AUC is the same as maximizing the normalized Gini coefficient (for a reference see the *Relation to other statistical measures* section in the Wikipedia entry: `https://en.wikipedia.org/wiki/Gini_coefficient`).

The metric can also be approximately expressed as the covariance of scaled prediction rank and scaled target value, resulting in a more understandable rank association measure (see Dmitriy Guller: `https://www.kaggle.com/competitions/porto-seguro-safe-driver-prediction/discussion/40576`).

From the point of view of the objective function, you can optimize for the binary log-loss (as you would do in a classification problem). Neither ROC-AUC nor the normalized Gini coefficient is differentiable, and they may be used only for metric evaluation on the validation set (for instance, for early stopping or for reducing the learning rate in a neural network). However, optimizing for the log-loss does not always improve the ROC-AUC and the normalized Gini coefficients and neither of them is directly differentiable.

There is actually a differentiable ROC-AUC approximation. You can read about how it works in Toon Calders, and Szymon Jaroszewicz *Efficient AUC Optimization for Classification*. European Conference on Principles of Data Mining and Knowledge Discovery. Springer, Berlin, Heidelberg, 2007: `https://link.springer.com/content/pdf/10.1007/978-3-540-74976-9_8.pdf`.

However, it seems that it is not necessary to use anything different from log-loss as an objective function and ROC-AUC or normalized Gini coefficient as an evaluation metric in the competition.

There are actually a few Python implementations for computing the normalized Gini coefficient among the Kaggle Notebooks. We have used here and suggest the work by CPMP (`https://www.kaggle.com/code/cpmpml/extremely-fast-gini-computation/notebook`) that uses Numba for speeding up computations: it is both exact and fast.

Exercise 2

In chapter 5 of *The Kaggle Book* (page 95 onward), we explained how to deal with competition metrics, especially if they are new and generally unknown.

As an exercise, can you find out how many competitions on Kaggle have used the normalized Gini coefficient as an evaluation metric?

Exercise Notes (write down any notes or workings that will help you):

Examining the top solution ideas from Michael Jahrer

Michael Jahrer (`https://www.kaggle.com/mjahrer`, competition Grandmaster and one of the winners of the Netflix Prize in the team "BellKor's Pragmatic Chaos") led the public leaderboard for a long time and by a fair margin during the competition and was declared the winner when the private solutions were finally disclosed.

Shortly after, in the discussion forum, he published a short summary of his solution that has become a reference for many Kagglers because of his smart usage of denoising autoencoders and neural networks (`https://www.kaggle.com/competitions/porto-seguro-safe-driver-prediction/discussion/44629`). Although Michael hasn't accompanied his post with any Python code regarding his solution (he described his coding work as an "old-school" and "low-level" one, being directly written in C++/CUDA with no Python), his writing is quite rich in references to what models he has used as well as their hyperparameters and architectures.

First, Michael explains that his solution is composed of a blend of six models (one LightGBM model and five neural networks). Moreover, since no advantage could be gained by weighting the contributions of each model to the blend (as well as doing linear and non-linear stacking), likely because of overfitting, he states that he resorted to just a blend of models (where all the models had equal weight) that have been built from different seeds.

Such insight makes the task much easier for us to replicate his approach, also because he also because he mentions that just having blended the LightGBM's results with one from the neural networks he built would have been enough to guarantee first place in the competition.

This insight will limit our exercise work to two good single models instead of a host of them. In addition, he mentioned having done little data processing, besides dropping some columns and one-hot encoding categorical features.

Building a LightGBM submission

Our exercise starts by working out a solution based on LightGBM. You can find the code already set for execution using Kaggle Notebooks at this address: `https://www.kaggle.com/code/lucamassaron/workbook-lgb`. Although we made the code readily available, we instead suggest you type or copy the code directly from the book and execute it cell by cell; understanding what each line of code does and personalizing the solution can make it perform even better.

When using LightGBM you don't have to, and should not, turn on any of the GPU or TPU accelerators. GPU acceleration could be helpful only if you have installed the GPU version of LightGBM. You can find working hints on how to install such a GPU-accelerated version on Kaggle Notebooks using this example: `https://www. kaggle.com/code/lucamassaron/gpu-accelerated-lightgbm`.

We start by importing key packages (NumPy, pandas, and Optuna for hyperparameter optimization, LightGBM, and some utility functions). We also define a configuration class and instantiate it. We will discuss the parameters defined in the configuration class during the exploration of the code as we progress. What is important to remark here is that by using a class containing all your parameters it will be easier for you to modify them in a consistent way along with the code. In the heat of competition, it is easy to forget to update a parameter that is referred to in multiple places in the code, and it is always difficult to set the parameters when they are dispersed among cells and functions. A configuration class can save you a lot of effort and spare you mistakes along the way:

```
import numpy as np
import pandas as pd
import optuna
import lightgbm as lgb
from path import Path
from sklearn.model_selection import StratifiedKFold

class Config:
    input_path = Path('../input/porto-seguro-safe-driver-prediction')
    optuna_lgb = False
    n_estimators = 1500
    early_stopping_round = 150
    cv_folds = 5
    random_state = 0
    params = {'objective': 'binary',
              'boosting_type': 'gbdt',
              'learning_rate': 0.01,
              'max_bin': 25,
              'num_leaves': 31,
              'min_child_samples': 1500,
```

```
                        'colsample_bytree': 0.7,
                        'subsample_freq': 1,
                        'subsample': 0.7,
                        'reg_alpha': 1.0,
                        'reg_lambda': 1.0,
                        'verbosity': 0,
                        'random_state': 0}

    config = Config()
```

The next step requires importing the training, test, and sample submission datasets. We do this using the pandas read_csv function. We also set the index of the uploaded DataFrames to the identifier (the id column) of each data example.

Since features that belong to similar groupings are tagged (using ind, reg, car, and calc tags in their labels) and also binary and categorical features are easy to locate (they use the bin and cat tags, respectively, in their labels), we can enumerate them and record them in lists:

```
    train = pd.read_csv(config.input_path / 'train.csv', index_col='id')
    test = pd.read_csv(config.input_path / 'test.csv', index_col='id')
    submission = pd.read_csv(config.input_path / 'sample_submission.csv',
    index_col='id')

    calc_features = [feat for feat in train.columns if "_calc" in feat]
    cat_features = [feat for feat in train.columns if "_cat" in feat]
```

Then, we just extract the target (a binary target of 0s and 1s) and remove it from the training dataset:

```
    target = train["target"]
    train = train.drop("target", axis="columns")
```

At this point, as pointed out by Michael Jahrer, we can drop the calc features. This idea has recurred a lot during the competition (https://www.kaggle.com/competitions/porto-seguro-safe-driver-prediction/discussion/41970), especially in notebooks, because it could be empirically verified that dropping them improved both the local cross-validation score and the public leaderboard score (as a general rule, it's important to keep track of both during feature selection). In addition, they also performed poorly in gradient boosting models (their importance is always below the average).

We can argue that, since they are engineered features, they do not contain new information in respect of their original features, but they just add noise to any model trained that comprises them:

```
train = train.drop(calc_features, axis="columns")
test = test.drop(calc_features, axis="columns")
```

Exercise 3

Based on the suggestions provided in *The Kaggle Book* on page 220 (*Using feature importance to evaluate your work*), as an exercise:

1. Code your own feature selection notebook for this competition.
2. Check what features should be kept and what should be discarded.

Exercise Notes (write down any notes or workings that will help you):

Categorical features are instead one-hot encoded. Because the same labels are present in the training and test datasets (the result of a careful train/test split between the two arranged by the Porto Seguro team), instead of the usual scikit-learn OneHotEncoder (https://scikit-learn. org/stable/modules/generated/sklearn.preprocessing.OneHotEncoder.html) we are going to use the pandas get_dummies function (https://pandas.pydata.org/docs/reference/api/ pandas.get_dummies.html). Since the pandas function may produce different encodings if the features and their levels differ from train to test set, we assert a check on the one-hot encoding, resulting in the same for both:

```
train = pd.get_dummies(train, columns=cat_features)
test = pd.get_dummies(test, columns=cat_features)

assert((train.columns==test.columns).all())
```

One-hot encoding the categorical features completes the data processing stage. We proceed to define our evaluation metric, the normalized Gini coefficient, as previously discussed. We will use the extremely fast Gini computation code proposed by CPMP, as mentioned before.

Since we are going to use a LightGBM model, we have to add a suitable wrapper (gini_lgb) to return to the GBM algorithm the evaluation of the training and the validation datasets in a form that can work with it (see https://lightgbm.readthedocs.io/en/latest/pythonapi/lightgbm. Booster.html?highlight=higher_better#lightgbm.Booster.eval – *Each evaluation function should accept two parameters: preds, eval_data, and return (eval_name, eval_result, is_higher_better) or list of such tuples*):

```
from numba import jit

@jit
def eval_gini(y_true, y_pred):
    y_true = np.asarray(y_true)
    y_true = y_true[np.argsort(y_pred)]
    ntrue = 0
    gini = 0
    delta = 0
    n = len(y_true)
    for i in range(n-1, -1, -1):
        y_i = y_true[i]
        ntrue += y_i
        gini += y_i * delta
```

```
        delta += 1 - y_i
    gini = 1 - 2 * gini / (ntrue * (n - ntrue))
    return gini


def gini_lgb(y_true, y_pred):
    eval_name = 'normalized_gini_coef'
    eval_result = eval_gini(y_true, y_pred)
    is_higher_better = True
    return eval_name, eval_result, is_higher_better
```

As for the training parameters, we found that the parameters suggested by Michael Jahrer in his post (https://www.kaggle.com/competitions/porto-seguro-safe-driver-prediction/discussion/44629) work perfectly.

You may also try to come up with the same parameters or similar performing ones by performing a search by Optuna (https://optuna.org/) if you set the optuna_lgb flag to True in the Config class. Here the optimization tries to find the best values for key parameters, such as the learning rate and the regularization parameters, based on a five-fold cross-validation test on training data. To speed up things, early stopping on the validation itself is taken into account (which, we are aware, could actually advantage picking some parameters that can better overfit the validation fold – a good alternative could be to remove the early stopping callback and keep a fixed number of rounds for the training):

```
if config.optuna_lgb:

    def objective(trial):
        params = {
        'learning_rate': trial.suggest_float("learning_rate", 0.01, 1.0),
        'num_leaves': trial.suggest_int("num_leaves", 3, 255),
        'min_child_samples': trial.suggest_int("min_child_samples",
                                    3, 3000),
        'colsample_bytree': trial.suggest_float("colsample_bytree",
                                    0.1, 1.0),
        'subsample_freq': trial.suggest_int("subsample_freq", 0, 10),
        'subsample': trial.suggest_float("subsample", 0.1, 1.0),
        'reg_alpha': trial.suggest_loguniform("reg_alpha", 1e-9, 10.0),
        'reg_lambda': trial.suggest_loguniform("reg_lambda", 1e-9, 10.0),
            }
```

```
        score = list()
        skf = StratifiedKFold(n_splits=config.cv_folds, shuffle=True,
                              random_state=config.random_state)

        for train_idx, valid_idx in skf.split(train, target):
            X_train = train.iloc[train_idx]
            y_train = target.iloc[train_idx]
            X_valid = train.iloc[valid_idx]
            y_valid = target.iloc[valid_idx]

            model = lgb.LGBMClassifier(**params,
                                    n_estimators=1500,
                                    early_stopping_round=150,
                                    force_row_wise=True)

            callbacks=[lgb.early_stopping(stopping_rounds=150,
                                        verbose=False)]
            model.fit(X_train, y_train,
                    eval_set=[(X_valid, y_valid)],
                    eval_metric=gini_lgb, callbacks=callbacks)

            score.append(
                model.best_score_['valid_0']['normalized_gini_coef'])

        return np.mean(score)

study = optuna.create_study(direction="maximize")
study.optimize(objective, n_trials=300)

print("Best Gini Normalized Score", study.best_value)
print("Best parameters", study.best_params)

params = {'objective': 'binary',
          'boosting_type': 'gbdt',
          'verbosity': 0,
          'random_state': 0}
```

```
        params.update(study.best_params)

  else:
        params = config.params
```

During the competition, Tilii tested feature elimination using Boruta (`https://github.com/scikit-learn-contrib/boruta_py`). You can find his kernel here: `https://www.kaggle.com/code/tilii7/boruta-feature-elimination/notebook`. As you can check, there is no `calc_` feature considered a confirmed feature by Boruta.

Exercise 4

In *The Kaggle Book*, we explain hyperparameter optimization (page 241 onward) and provide some key hyperparameters for the LightGBM model.

As an exercise:

Try to improve the hyperparameter search by Optuna by reducing or increasing the explored parameters where you deem it necessary, and also try alternative optimization methods, such as the random search or the halving search from scikit-learn (pages 245–246).

Exercise Notes (write down any notes or workings that will help you):

Once we have got our best parameters (or we simply try Jahrer's ones), we are ready to train and predict. Our strategy, as suggested by the best solution, is to train a model on each cross-validation fold and use that fold to contribute to an average of test predictions. The snippet of code will produce both the test predictions and the out-of-fold predictions on the training dataset, which will be useful for figuring out how to ensemble the results:

```python
preds = np.zeros(len(test))
oof = np.zeros(len(train))
metric_evaluations = list()

skf = StratifiedKFold(n_splits=config.cv_folds, shuffle=True, random_
state=config.random_state)

for idx, (train_idx, valid_idx) in enumerate(skf.split(train,
                                                       target)):
    print(f"CV fold {idx}")
    X_train, y_train = train.iloc[train_idx], target.iloc[train_idx]
    X_valid, y_valid = train.iloc[valid_idx], target.iloc[valid_idx]

    model = lgb.LGBMClassifier(**params,
                               n_estimators=config.n_estimators,
                     early_stopping_round=config.early_stopping_round,
                               force_row_wise=True)

    callbacks=[lgb.early_stopping(stopping_rounds=150),
             lgb.log_evaluation(period=100, show_stdv=False)]

    model.fit(X_train, y_train,
             eval_set=[(X_valid, y_valid)],
             eval_metric=gini_lgb, callbacks=callbacks)
    metric_evaluations.append(
             model.best_score_['valid_0']['normalized_gini_coef'])
    preds += (model.predict_proba(test,
             num_iteration=model.best_iteration_)[:,1]
             / skf.n_splits)

    oof[valid_idx] = model.predict_proba(X_valid,
                     num_iteration=model.best_iteration_)[:,1]
```

The model training shouldn't take too long. In the end you can get the reported Normalized Gini Coefficient obtained during the cross-validation procedure:

```
print(f"LightGBM CV normalized Gini coefficient:
        {np.mean(metric_evaluations):0.3f}
        ({np.std(metric_evaluations):0.3f})")
```

The results are quite encouraging because the average score is 0.289 and the standard deviation of the values is quite small:

```
LightGBM CV Gini Normalized Score: 0.289 (0.015)
```

All that is left is to save the out-of-fold and test predictions as a submission and to verify the results on the public and private leaderboards:

```
submission['target'] = preds
submission.to_csv('lgb_submission.csv')

oofs = pd.DataFrame({'id':train_index, 'target':oof})
oofs.to_csv('lgb_oof.csv', index=False)
```

The obtained public score should be around 0.28442. The associated private score is about 0.29121, placing you in the 29th position on the final leaderboard. A quite good result, but we still have to blend it with a different model, a neural network.

Bagging the training set (i.e., taking multiple bootstraps of the training data and training multiple models based on the bootstraps) should increase the performance, although, as Michael Jahrer himself noted in his post, not all that much.

Setting up a denoising autoencoder and a DNN

The next step is to set up a **denoising autoencoder** (DAE) and a neural network that can learn and predict from it. You can find the running code in this notebook: https://www.kaggle.com/code/lucamassaron/workbook-dae. The notebook can be run in GPU mode (it will therefore be speedier if you turn on the accelerators in the Kaggle Notebook), but it can also run in CPU mode with some slight modifications.

 You can read more about denoising autoencoders being used in Kaggle competitions in *The Kaggle Book*, from page 230 onward.

Actually there are no examples that reproduce Michael Jahrer's approach in the competition using DAEs, so we took an example from a TensorFlow implementation in another competition coded by OsciiArt (https://www.kaggle.com/code/osciiart/denoising-autoencoder).

Here we start by importing all the necessary packages, especially TensorFlow and Keras. Since we are going to create multiple neural networks, we point out to TensorFlow not to use all the GPU memory available by using the experimental set_memory_growth command. This will help us avoid having memory overflow problems along the way. We also record the Leaky ReLu activation as a custom one, so we can just mention it as an activation by a string in the Keras layers:

```python
import numpy as np
import pandas as pd
from matplotlib import pyplot as plt
from path import Path
import gc

import optuna

from sklearn.model_selection import StratifiedKFold

from scipy.special import erfinv

import tensorflow as tf
gpus = tf.config.experimental.list_physical_devices('GPU')
for gpu in gpus:
    tf.config.experimental.set_memory_growth(gpu, True)

from tensorflow import keras
from tensorflow.keras import backend as K
from tensorflow.keras.layers import Input, Dense, BatchNormalization,
Dropout
from tensorflow.keras.models import Model, load_model
from tensorflow.keras.callbacks import EarlyStopping, ReduceLROnPlateau
from tensorflow.keras.regularizers import l2
from tensorflow.keras.metrics import AUC

from tensorflow.keras.utils import get_custom_objects
```

```
from tensorflow.keras.layers import Activation, LeakyReLU
get_custom_objects().update({'leaky-relu':
Activation(LeakyReLU(alpha=0.2))})
```

Related to our intention of creating multiple neural networks without running out of memory, we also define a simple function for cleaning the memory in GPU and removing models that are no longer needed:

```
def gpu_cleanup(objects):
    if objects:
        del(objects)
    K.clear_session()
    gc.collect()
```

We also reconfigure the Config class to take into account multiple parameters related to the denoising autoencoder and the neural network. As previously stated about the LightGBM, having all the parameters in a unique place simplifies the process when you have to change them in a consistent way:

```
class Config:
    input_path = Path('../input/porto-seguro-safe-driver-prediction')
    dae_batch_size = 128
    dae_num_epoch = 50
    dae_architecture = [1500, 1500, 1500]
    reuse_autoencoder = False

    batch_size = 128
    num_epoch = 150
    units = [64, 32]
    input_dropout=0.06
    dropout=0.08
    regL2=0.09
    activation='selu'

    cv_folds = 5
    nas = False
    random_state = 0

config = Config()
```

As shown previously, we load the datasets and proceed to process the features by removing the calc features and one-hot encoding the categorical ones. We leave missing cases valued at -1, as Michael Jahrer pointed out in his solution:

```python
train = pd.read_csv(config.input_path / 'train.csv', index_col='id')
test = pd.read_csv(config.input_path / 'test.csv', index_col='id')
submission = pd.read_csv(config.input_path / 'sample_submission.csv',
index_col='id')

calc_features = [feat for feat in train.columns if "_calc" in feat]
cat_features = [feat for feat in train.columns if "_cat" in feat]
target = train["target"]
train = train.drop("target", axis="columns")

train = train.drop(calc_features, axis="columns")
test = test.drop(calc_features, axis="columns")
train = pd.get_dummies(train, columns=cat_features)
test = pd.get_dummies(test, columns=cat_features)

assert((train.columns==test.columns).all())
```

However, since we are dealing with neural networks, we have to normalize all the features that are not binary or one-hot-encoded categorical. Normalization implies rescaling (setting a limited range of values) and centering (your distribution will be centered to a certain value, usually zero)

Normalization will allow the optimization algorithm of both the autoencoder and the neural network to converge to a good solution faster because it reduces the danger of oscillations of the loss function during the optimization. In addition, normalization facilitates the propagation of the input through the activation functions.

Instead of using statistical normalization (bringing your distribution of values to have zero mean and unit standard deviation), GaussRank is a procedure that also allows the modification of the distribution of the variables into a transformed Gaussian one. As also stated in some papers, such as in *Batch Normalization: Accelerating Deep Network Training by Reducing Internal Covariate Shift* (https://arxiv.org/pdf/1502.03167.pdf), neural networks perform even better if you provide them with a Gaussian input. Accordingly to this NVIDIA blog post, https://developer.nvidia.com/blog/gauss-rank-transformation-is-100x-faster-with-rapids-and-cupy/, GaussRank works most of the time, except when features are already normally distributed or are extremely asymmetrical (in such cases applying the transformation may lead to worsened performance):

```
print("Applying GaussRank to columns: ", end='')
to_normalize = list()
for k, col in enumerate(train.columns):
    if '_bin' not in col and '_cat' not in col and '_missing' not in col:
        to_normalize.append(col)
print(to_normalize)

def to_gauss(x): return np.sqrt(2) * erfinv(x)

def normalize(data, norm_cols):
    n = data.shape[0]
    for col in norm_cols:
        sorted_idx = data[col].sort_values().index.tolist()
        uniform = np.linspace(start=-0.99, stop=0.99, num=n)
        normal = to_gauss(uniform)
        normalized_col = pd.Series(index=sorted_idx, data=normal)
        data[col] = normalized_col
    return data

train = normalize(train, to_normalize)
test = normalize(test, to_normalize)
```

We can apply the GaussRank transformation separately on the train and test features on all the numeric features of our dataset:

```
Applying GaussRank to columns: ['ps_ind_01', 'ps_ind_03', 'ps_ind_14',
'ps_ind_15', 'ps_reg_01', 'ps_reg_02', 'ps_reg_03', 'ps_car_11', 'ps_
car_12', 'ps_car_13', 'ps_car_14', 'ps_car_15']
```

When normalizing the features, we simply turn our data into a NumPy array of float32 values, the ideal input for a GPU:

```
features = train.columns
train_index = train.index
test_index = test.index

train = train.values.astype(np.float32)
test = test.values.astype(np.float32)
```

Next, we just prepare some useful functions, such as the evaluation function, the normalized Gini coefficient (based on the code described before), and a plotting function that helpfully represents a Keras model history of fitting on both training and validation sets:

```python
def plot_keras_history(history, measures):
    rows = len(measures) // 2 + len(measures) % 2
    fig, panels = plt.subplots(rows, 2, figsize=(15, 5))
    plt.subplots_adjust(top = 0.99, bottom=0.01,
                            hspace=0.4, wspace=0.2)
    try:
        panels = [item for sublist in panels for item in sublist]
    except:
        pass
    for k, measure in enumerate(measures):
        panel = panels[k]
        panel.set_title(measure + ' history')
        panel.plot(history.epoch, history.history[measure],
                    label="Train "+measure)
        try:
            panel.plot(history.epoch,
                        history.history["val_"+measure],
                        label="Validation "+measure)
        except:
            pass
        panel.set(xlabel='epochs', ylabel=measure)
        panel.legend()

    plt.show(fig)

from numba import jit

@jit
def eval_gini(y_true, y_pred):
    y_true = np.asarray(y_true)
    y_true = y_true[np.argsort(y_pred)]
    ntrue = 0
    gini = 0
    delta = 0
```

```
    n = len(y_true)
    for i in range(n-1, -1, -1):
        y_i = y_true[i]
        ntrue += y_i
        gini += y_i * delta
        delta += 1 - y_i
    gini = 1 - 2 * gini / (ntrue * (n - ntrue))
    return gini
```

The next functions are actually a bit more complex and more related to the functioning of both the denoising autoencoder and the supervised neural network. The batch_generator is a function that will create a generator that provides shuffled chunks of the data based on batch size. It isn't actually used as a standalone generator but as part of a more complex batch generator that we will soon describe, the mixup_generator:

```
def batch_generator(x, batch_size, shuffle=True, random_state=None):
    batch_index = 0
    n = x.shape[0]
    while True:
        if batch_index == 0:
            index_array = np.arange(n)
            if shuffle:
                np.random.seed(seed=random_state)
                index_array = np.random.permutation(n)

        current_index = (batch_index * batch_size) % n
        if n >= current_index + batch_size:
            current_batch_size = batch_size
            batch_index += 1
        else:
            current_batch_size = n - current_index
            batch_index = 0

        batch = x[index_array[current_index: current_index + current_
batch_size]]

        yield batch
```

The `mixup_generator` is a generator that returns batches of data whose values have been partially swapped to create some noise and augment the data to avoid the DAE overfitting to the training dataset. You can look at this generator as a way to inject random values into the dataset and create many more examples to be used for training. It works based on a swap rate, fixed at 15%, of features as suggested by Michael Jahrer, implying that at every batch, you will have 15% of the random values in the sample. It is also important to point out that having the random values picked randomly from the very same features means that the replacing random values are not completely random, since they are from the same distribution of the original features.

The function generates two distinct batches of data, one to be released to the model and another to be used as a source for the value to be swapped in the batch to be released. Based on a random choice, whose base probability is the swap rate, at each batch, a certain number of features will be swapped between the two batches.

This means that the DAE cannot always rely on the same features (since they can be randomly swapped from time to time) but instead has to concentrate on the whole of the features (something similar to dropout in a certain sense) to find relationships between them and correctly reconstruct the data at the end of the process:

```python
def mixup_generator(X, batch_size, swaprate=0.15, shuffle=True, random_
state=None):
    if random_state is None:
        random_state = np.randint(0, 999)
    num_features = X.shape[1]
    num_swaps = int(num_features * swaprate)
    generator_a = batch_generator(X, batch_size, shuffle,
                                  random_state)
    generator_b = batch_generator(X, batch_size, shuffle,
                                  random_state + 1)

    while True:
        batch = next(generator_a)
        mixed_batch = batch.copy()
        effective_batch_size = batch.shape[0]
        alternative_batch = next(generator_b)
        assert((batch != alternative_batch).any())
        for i in range(effective_batch_size):
            swap_idx = np.random.choice(num_features, num_swaps,
```

```
                                    replace=False)
          mixed_batch[i, swap_idx] = alternative_batch[i, swap_idx]
      yield (mixed_batch, batch)
```

The get_DAE is the function that builds the denoising autoencoder. It accepts a parameter for defining the architecture, which in our case has been set to three layers of 1,500 nodes each (as suggested by Michael Jahrer's solution). The first layer should act as an encoder, the second is a bottleneck layer ideally containing the latent features capable of expressing the information in the data, and the last layer is a decoding layer capable of reconstructing the initial input data. The three layers have a relu activation function, no bias, and each one is followed by a batch normalization layer. The final output with the reconstructed input data has a linear activation. The training is optimized using an adam optimizer with standard settings (the optimized cost function is the mean squared error – mse):

```
def get_DAE(X, architecture=[1500, 1500, 1500]):
    features = X.shape[1]
    inputs = Input((features,))
    for i, nodes in enumerate(architecture):
        layer = Dense(nodes, activation='relu',
                      use_bias=False, name=f"code_{i+1}")
        if i==0:
            x = layer(inputs)
        else:
            x = layer(x)
        x = BatchNormalization()(x)
    outputs = Dense(features, activation='linear')(x)
    model = Model(inputs=inputs, outputs=outputs)
    model.compile(optimizer='adam', loss='mse',
                  metrics=['mse', 'mae'])
    return model
```

The extract_dae_features function is reported here only for educational purposes. The function helps in the extraction of the values of specific layers of the trained denoising autoencoder. The extraction works by building a new model, combining the DAE input layer and the desired output one. A simple predict will then extract the values we need (the predict also allows us to fix the preferred batch size in order to fit any memory requirement).

In the case of the competition, given the number of observations and the number of features to be taken out from the autoencoder, if we were to use this function, the resulting dense matrix would be too large to be handled by the memory of a Kaggle Notebook. For this reason, our strategy won't be to transform the original data into the autoencoder node values of the bottleneck layer but to instead fuse the autoencoder with its frozen layers up to the bottleneck with the supervised neural network, as we will be discussing soon:

```python
def extract_dae_features(autoencoder, X, layers=[3], batch_size=128):
    data = []
    for layer in layers:
        if layer==0:
            data.append(X)
        else:
            get_layer_output = Model([autoencoder.layers[0].input],
                                     [autoencoder.layers[layer].output])
            layer_output = get_layer_output.predict(X,
                                                     batch_size= batch_size)
            data.append(layer_output)
    data = np.hstack(data)
    return data
```

To complete the work with the DAE, we have a final function wrapping all the previous ones into an unsupervised training procedure (at least partially unsupervised since there is an early stop monitor set on a validation set). The function sets up the mix-up generator, creates the denoising autoencoder architecture, and then trains it, monitoring its fit on a validation set for an early stop if there are signs of overfitting. Finally, before returning the trained DAE, it plots a graph of the training and validation fit and stores the model on disk.

Even if we try to fix a seed on this model, contrary to the LightGBM model, the results are extremely variable, and they may influence the final ensemble results. Though the result will be a high scoring one, it may land higher or lower on the public and private leaderboards (public results are very correlated to the private leaderboard) and it will be easy for you to always pick up the best final submission based on its public results:

```python
def autoencoder_fitting(X_train, X_valid, filename='dae',
                        random_state=None, suppress_output=False):
    if suppress_output:
        verbose = 0
```

```
    else:
        verbose = 2
        print("Fitting a denoising autoencoder")

    tf.random.set_seed(seed=random_state)
    generator = mixup_generator(X_train,
                                batch_size=config.dae_batch_size,
                                swaprate=0.15,
                                random_state=config.random_state)

    dae = get_DAE(X_train, architecture=config.dae_architecture)
    steps_per_epoch = np.ceil(X_train.shape[0] /
                              config.dae_batch_size)

    early_stopping = EarlyStopping(monitor='val_mse',
                                   mode='min',
                                   patience=5,
                                   restore_best_weights=True,
                                   verbose=0)

    history = dae.fit(generator,
                      steps_per_epoch=steps_per_epoch,
                      epochs=config.dae_num_epoch,
                      validation_data=(X_valid, X_valid),
                      callbacks=[early_stopping],
                      verbose=verbose)

    if not suppress_output: plot_keras_history(history,
                                               measures=['mse', 'mae'])

    dae.save(filename)

    return dae
```

Having dealt with the DAE, we take the chance also to define the supervised neural model down the line that should predict our claim expectations. As a first step, we define a function to define a single layer of the work:

- Random normal initialization, since empirically it has been found to converge to better results in this problem.
- A dense layer with L2 regularization and a customizable activation function.
- A tunable dropout layer, which can be easily included or excluded from the architecture.

Here is the code for creating the dense blocks:

```python
def dense_blocks(x, units, activation, regL2, dropout):
    kernel_initializer = keras.initializers.RandomNormal(mean=0.0,
                              stddev=0.1, seed=config.random_state)
    for k, layer_units in enumerate(units):
        if regL2 > 0:
            x = Dense(layer_units, activation=activation,
                    kernel_initializer=kernel_initializer,
                    kernel_regularizer=l2(regL2))(x)
        else:
            x = Dense(layer_units,
                    kernel_initializer=kernel_initializer,
                    activation=activation)(x)
        if dropout > 0:
            x = Dropout(dropout)(x)
    return x
```

As you may have already noticed, the function defining the single layer is quite customizable. The same goes for the wrapper architecture function, taking inputs for the number of layers and units in them, dropout probabilities, regularization, and activation type. The idea is to be able to run a **neural architecture search** (**NAS**) and figure out what configuration should perform better in our problem.

As a final note on the function, among the inputs, it is required to provide the trained DAE because its inputs are used as the neural network model inputs while its first layers are connected to the DAE's bottleneck layer (the middle layer in the DAE architecture). In such a way we are de facto concatenating the two models into one (although the DAE weights are frozen anyway and not trainable).

This solution has been devised to avoid having to transform all your training data and instead only the single batches that the neural network is processing, thus saving memory in the system:

```python
def dnn_model(dae, units=[4500, 1000, 1000],
              input_dropout=0.1, dropout=0.5,
              regL2=0.05,
              activation='relu'):

    inputs = dae.get_layer("code_2").output
    if input_dropout > 0:
        x = Dropout(input_dropout)(inputs)
    else:
        x = tf.keras.layers.Layer()(inputs)
    x = dense_blocks(x, units, activation, regL2, dropout)
    outputs = Dense(1, activation='sigmoid')(x)

    model = Model(inputs=dae.input, outputs=outputs)
    model.compile(optimizer=keras.optimizers.Adam(learning_rate=0.001),
                  loss=keras.losses.binary_crossentropy,
                  metrics=[AUC(name='auc')])
    return model
```

We conclude with a wrapper for the training process, including all the steps in order to train the entire pipeline on a cross-validation fold:

```python
def model_fitting(X_train, y_train, X_valid, y_valid, autoencoder,
                  filename, random_state=None, suppress_output=False):
    if suppress_output:
        verbose = 0
    else:
        verbose = 2
        print("Fitting model")

    early_stopping = EarlyStopping(monitor='val_auc',
                                   mode='max',
                                   patience=10,
                                   restore_best_weights=True,
                                   verbose=0)
```

```
        rlrop = ReduceLROnPlateau(monitor='val_auc',
                                  mode='max',
                                  patience=2,
                                  factor=0.75,
                                  verbose=0)


    tf.random.set_seed(seed=random_state)


    model = dnn_model(autoencoder,
                      units=config.units,
                      input_dropout=config.input_dropout,
                      dropout=config.dropout,
                      regL2=config.regL2,
                      activation=config.activation)


    history = model.fit(X_train, y_train,
                        epochs=config.num_epoch,
                        batch_size=config.batch_size,
                        validation_data=(X_valid, y_valid),
                        callbacks=[early_stopping, rlrop],
                        shuffle=True,
                        verbose=verbose)


    model.save(filename)


    if not suppress_output:
        plot_keras_history(history, measures=['loss', 'auc'])


    return model, history
```

Since our DAE implementation is surely different from Jahrer's, although the idea behind it is the same, we cannot rely completely on his observations on the architecture of the supervised neural network, and we have to look for the ideal indications as we have been looking for the best hyperparameters in the LightGBM model. Using Optuna and leveraging the multiple parameters that we set to configure the network's architecture, we can run this code snippet for some hours and get an idea about what could work better.

In our experiments we found that:

- We should use a two-layer network with fewer nodes, 64 and 32 respectively.

- Input dropout, dropout between layers, and some L2 regularization do help.

- It is better to use the SELU activation function.

Here is the code snippet for running the entire optimization experiments:

```python
if config.nas is True:
    def evaluate():
        metric_evaluations = list()

        skf = StratifiedKFold(n_splits=config.cv_folds, shuffle=True,
random_state=config.random_state)

        for k, (train_idx, valid_idx) in enumerate(skf.split(train,
target)):

            X_train, y_train = train[train_idx, :], target[train_idx]
            X_valid, y_valid = train[valid_idx, :], target[valid_idx]

            if config.reuse_autoencoder:
                autoencoder = load_model(f"./dae_fold_{k}")
            else:
                autoencoder = autoencoder_fitting(X_train, X_valid,
                                                  filename=f'./dae_fold_
{k}',
                                                  random_state=config.
random_state,
                                                  suppress_output=True)

            model, _ = model_fitting(X_train, y_train, X_valid, y_valid,
                                     autoencoder=autoencoder,
                                     filename=f"dnn_model_fold_{k}",
                                     random_state=config.random_state,
                                     suppress_output=True)

            val_preds = model.predict(X_valid, batch_size=128, verbose=0)
```

```
            best_score = eval_gini(y_true=y_valid, y_pred=np.ravel(val_
preds))
            metric_evaluations.append(best_score)

            gpu_cleanup([autoencoder, model])

        return np.mean(metric_evaluations)

    def objective(trial):
        params = {
                'first_layer': trial.suggest_categorical("first_layer",
[8, 16, 32, 64, 128, 256, 512]),
                'second_layer': trial.suggest_categorical("second_layer",
[0, 8, 16, 32, 64, 128, 256]),
                'third_layer': trial.suggest_categorical("third_layer",
[0, 8, 16, 32, 64, 128, 256]),
                'input_dropout': trial.suggest_float("input_dropout", 0.0,
0.5),
                'dropout': trial.suggest_float("dropout", 0.0, 0.5),
                'regL2': trial.suggest_uniform("regL2", 0.0, 0.1),
                'activation': trial.suggest_categorical("activation",
['relu', 'leaky-relu', 'selu'])
        }

        config.units = [nodes for nodes in [params['first_layer'],
params['second_layer'], params['third_layer']] if nodes > 0]
        config.input_dropout = params['input_dropout']
        config.dropout = params['dropout']
        config.regL2 = params['regL2']
        config.activation = params['activation']

        return evaluate()

    study = optuna.create_study(direction="maximize")
    study.optimize(objective, n_trials=60)

    print("Best Gini Normalized Score", study.best_value)
    print("Best parameters", study.best_params)
```

```
    config.units = [nodes for nodes in [study.best_params['first_layer'],
study.best_params['second_layer'], study.best_params['third_layer']] if
nodes > 0]
    config.input_dropout = study.best_params['input_dropout']
    config.dropout = study.best_params['dropout']
    config.regL2 = study.best_params['regL2']
    config.activation = study.best_params['activation']
```

Exercise 5

If you are looking for more information about NAS, you can have a look at *The Kaggle Book*, on page 276 onward. In the case of the DAE and the supervised neural network, it is critical to look for the best architecture since we are implementing something surely different from Michael Jahrer's solution.

As an exercise, try to improve the hyperparameter search by using KerasTuner (to be found on page 285 onward in *The Kaggle Book*), a fast solution for optimizing neural networks that includes the contribution of François Chollet, the creator of Keras.

Exercise Notes (write down any notes or workings that will help you):

Having finally set everything ready, we are set to start the training. In about one hour, on a Kaggle Notebook with GPU, you can obtain complete test and out-of-fold predictions:

```python
preds = np.zeros(len(test))
oof = np.zeros(len(train))
metric_evaluations = list()
skf = StratifiedKFold(n_splits=config.cv_folds, shuffle=True, random_
state=config.random_state)

for k, (train_idx, valid_idx) in enumerate(skf.split(train, target)):
    print(f"CV fold {k}")

    X_train, y_train = train[train_idx, :], target[train_idx]
    X_valid, y_valid = train[valid_idx, :], target[valid_idx]

    if config.reuse_autoencoder:
        print("restoring previously trained dae")
        autoencoder = load_model(f"./dae_fold_{k}")
    else:
        autoencoder = autoencoder_fitting(X_train, X_valid,
                                    filename=f'./dae_fold_{k}',
                                    random_state=config.random_state)

    model, history = model_fitting(X_train, y_train, X_valid, y_valid,
                              autoencoder=autoencoder,
                              filename=f"dnn_model_fold_{k}",
                              random_state=config.random_state)

    val_preds = model.predict(X_valid, batch_size=128)
    best_score = eval_gini(y_true=y_valid,
                       y_pred=np.ravel(val_preds))

    best_epoch = np.argmax(history.history['val_auc']) + 1
    print(f"[best epoch is {best_epoch}]\tvalidation_0-gini_dnn: {best_
score:0.5f}\n")

    metric_evaluations.append(best_score)
    preds += (model.predict(test, batch_size=128).ravel() /
```

```
                    skf.n_splits)
    oof[valid_idx] = model.predict(X_valid, batch_size=128).ravel()


    gpu_cleanup([autoencoder, model])
```

As we did with the LighGBM model, we can get an idea of the results by looking at the average fold normalized Gini coefficient:

```
print(f"DNN CV normalized Gini coefficient: {np.mean(metric_
evaluations):0.3f} ({np.std(metric_evaluations):0.3f})")
```

The results won't be quite in line with what was previously obtained using the LightGBM:

```
DNN CV Gini Normalized Score: 0.276 (0.015)
```

Producing the submission and submitting it will result in a public score of about 0.27737 and a private score of about 0.28471 (results may vary wildly as we previously mentioned) – not quite a high score:

```
submission['target'] = preds
submission.to_csv('dnn_submission.csv')


oofs = pd.DataFrame({'id':train_index, 'target':oof})
oofs.to_csv('dnn_oof.csv', index=False)
```

The scarce results from the neural network seem to confirm the idea that neural networks underperform in tabular problems. As Kagglers, anyway, we know that all models are useful for a successful placing on the leaderboard; we just need to figure out how to best use them. Surely, a neural network feed with an autoencoder has worked out a solution less affected by noise in data and elaborated the information in a different way than a GBM.

Ensembling the results

Now, having two models, what's left is to mix them together and see if we can improve the results. As suggested by Jahrer we go straight for a blend of them, but we do not limit ourselves to producing just an average of the two (since our approach in the end has slightly differed from Jahrer's one) and we will also try to get optimal weights for the blend. We start importing the out-of-fold predictions and get our evaluation function ready:

```
import pandas as pd
import numpy as np
```

```
from numba import jit

@jit
def eval_gini(y_true, y_pred):
    y_true = np.asarray(y_true)
    y_true = y_true[np.argsort(y_pred)]
    ntrue = 0
    gini = 0
    delta = 0
    n = len(y_true)
    for i in range(n-1, -1, -1):
        y_i = y_true[i]
        ntrue += y_i
        gini += y_i * delta
        delta += 1 - y_i
    gini = 1 - 2 * gini / (ntrue * (n - ntrue))
    return gini

lgb_oof = pd.read_csv("../input/workbook-lgb/lgb_oof.csv")
dnn_oof = pd.read_csv("../input/workbook-dae/dnn_oof.csv")

target = pd.read_csv("../input/porto-seguro-safe-driver-prediction/train.
csv", usecols=['id','target'])
```

Once done, we convert the out-of-fold predictions of the LightGBM and the predictions of the neural network into ranks. We are doing so because the normalized Gini coefficient is based on rankings (as a ROC-AUC evaluation would be) and consequently blending rankings works better than blending the predicted probabilities::

```
lgb_oof_ranks = (lgb_oof.target.rank() / len(lgb_oof))
dnn_oof_ranks = (dnn_oof.target.rank() / len(dnn_oof))
```

Now we just test if, by combining the two models using different weights, we can get a better evaluation of the out-of-fold data:

```
baseline = eval_gini(y_true=target.target, y_pred=lgb_oof_ranks)

print(f"starting from a oof lgb baseline {baseline:0.5f}\n")

best_alpha = 1.0
```

```
for alpha in [0.1, 0.2, 0.3, 0.4, 0.5, 0.6, 0.7, 0.8, 0.9]:
    ensemble = alpha * lgb_oof_ranks + (1.0 - alpha) * dnn_oof_ranks
    score = eval_gini(y_true=target.target, y_pred=ensemble)
    print(f"lgd={alpha:0.1f} dnn={(1.0 - alpha):0.1f} -> {score:0.5f}")

    if score > baseline:
        baseline = score
        best_alpha = alpha

print(f"\nBest alpha is {best_alpha:0.1f}")
```

When ready, by running the snippet we can get interesting results:

```
starting from a oof lgb baseline 0.28850

lgd=0.1 dnn=0.9 -> 0.27352
lgd=0.2 dnn=0.8 -> 0.27744
lgd=0.3 dnn=0.7 -> 0.28084
lgd=0.4 dnn=0.6 -> 0.28368
lgd=0.5 dnn=0.5 -> 0.28595
lgd=0.6 dnn=0.4 -> 0.28763
lgd=0.7 dnn=0.3 -> 0.28873
lgd=0.8 dnn=0.2 -> 0.28923
lgd=0.9 dnn=0.1 -> 0.28916

Best alpha is 0.8
```

It seems that blending a strong weight (0.8) on the LightGBM model and a weaker one (0.2) on the neural network will bring an even better-performing model. We immediately try this hypothesis by setting a blend of the same weights for the models and the ideal weights that we have found:

```
lgb_submission = pd.read_csv("../input/workbook-lgb/lgb_submission.csv")
dnn_submission = pd.read_csv("../input/workbook-dae/dnn_submission.csv")

submission = pd.read_csv(
"../input/porto-seguro-safe-driver-prediction/sample_submission.csv")
```

First, we try the equal weights solution, which was the strategy used by Michael Jahrer:

```
lgb_ranks = (lgb_submission.target.rank() / len(lgb_submission))
dnn_ranks = (dnn_submission.target.rank() / len(dnn_submission))
submission.target = lgb_ranks * 0.5 + dnn_ranks * 0.5

submission.to_csv("equal_blend_rank.csv", index=False)
```

It leads to a public score of 0.28393 and a private score of 0.29093, which is around 50th position on the final leaderboard, a bit far from our expectations. Now let's try using the weights that the out-of-fold predictions helped us to find:

```
lgb_ranks = (lgb_submission.target.rank() / len(lgb_submission))
dnn_ranks = (dnn_submission.target.rank() / len(dnn_submission))

submission.target = lgb_ranks * best_alpha +  dnn_ranks * (1.0 - best_
alpha)

submission.to_csv("blend_rank.csv", index=False)
```

Here the results lead to a public score of 0.28502 and a private score of 0.29192, which turns out to be around the seventh position on the final leaderboard. A much better result indeed because the LightGBM is a good model, but it is probably missing some nuances in the data that can be provided by adding some information from the neural network trained on the denoised data.

Exercise 6

As pointed out by CPMP in their solution (`https://www.kaggle.com/competitions/porto-seguro-safe-driver-prediction/discussion/44614`), depending on how to build your cross-validation, you can experience a *"huge variation of Gini scores among folds."* For this reason, CPMP suggests decreasing the variance of the estimates by using many different seeds for multiple cross-validations and averaging the results.

As an exercise, try to modify the code we used to create more stable predictions, especially for the denoising autoencoder.

Exercise Notes (write down any notes or workings that will help you):

Summary

In this first chapter, you have dealt with a classical tabular competition. By reading the notebooks and discussions of the competition, we have come up with a simple solution involving just two models that can be easily blended. In particular, we have offered an example of how to use a denoising autoencoder in order to produce alternative data processing, particularly useful when operating with neural networks for tabular data. By understanding and replicating solutions from past competitions, you can quickly build up your core competencies on Kaggle competitions and quickly become able to perform consistently higher in more recent competitions and challenges.

In the next chapter, we will explore another tabular competition from Kaggle, this time revolving around a complex prediction problem with time series.

Join our book's Discord space

Join our Discord community to meet like-minded people and learn alongside more than 2000 members at:

`https://packt.link/KaggleDiscord`

2

The Makridakis Competitions – M5 on Kaggle for Accuracy and Uncertainty

Since 1982, Spyros Makridakis (`https://mofc.unic.ac.cy/dr-spyros-makridakis/https://mofc.unic.ac.cy/dr-spyros-makridakis/`) has involved groups of researchers from all over the world in forecasting challenges, called M Competitions, in order to conduct comparisons of the efficacy of existing and new forecasting methods against different prediction problems. For this reason, M Competitions have always been completely open to both academics and practitioners. The competitions are probably the most cited and referenced event in the forecasting community and they have always highlighted the changing state of the art in forecasting methods. Each previous M Competition has provided both researchers and practitioners not only with useful data to train and test their forecasting tools but also with a series of discoveries and approaches revolutionizing the way forecasting is done.

The recent M5 Competition (the M6 is running as this chapter is being written) was held on Kaggle, and it proved particularly significant in remarking on the usefulness of gradient-boosting methods when trying to solve a host of volume forecasts of retail products. In this chapter, focusing on the accuracy track, we deal with a time series problem from Kaggle competitions, and by replicating one of the top-ranking, yet simplest and most clear solutions, we intend to provide our readers with code and ideas to successfully handle any future forecasting competition that may appear on Kaggle.

Apart from the competition pages, we found a lot of information regarding the competition and its dynamics in the following papers from the International Journal of Forecasting:

- Makridakis, Spyros, Evangelos Spiliotis, and Vassilios Assimakopoulos. *The M5 competition: Background, organization, and implementation.* International Journal of Forecasting (2021).
- Makridakis, Spyros, Evangelos Spiliotis, and Vassilios Assimakopoulos. *M5 accuracy competition: Results, findings, and conclusions.* International Journal of Forecasting (2022).
- Makridakis, Spyros, et al. *The M5 Uncertainty competition: Results, findings and conclusions.* International Journal of Forecasting (2021).

In this chapter, you will learn:

- The competition time-series data and evaluation metric
- Computing predictions for specific dates and time horizons
- Assembling the predictions from different time windows

All the code files for this chapter can be found at `https://packt.link/kwbchp2`

Understanding the competition and the data

The competition (`https://www.kaggle.com/competitions/m5-forecasting-accuracy`) ran from March to June 2020 and over 7,000 participants took part in it on Kaggle. The organizers arranged it into two separate tracks, one for point-wise prediction (accuracy track) and another one for estimating reliable values at different confidence intervals (uncertainty track). Our focus in this chapter will be to try to replicate one of the best submissions for the accuracy track and also pave the way for the uncertainty track (since it is based on the predictions of the accuracy one).

Walmart provided the data. It consisted of 42,840 daily sales time series of items hierarchically arranged into departments, categories, and stores spread in three U.S. states (the time series are somewhat correlated with each other). Along with the sales, Walmart also provided accompanying information (exogenous variables, usually not often provided in forecasting problems) such as the prices of items, some calendar information, associated promotions, or the presence of other events affecting the sales.

Apart from Kaggle, the data is available, together with the datasets from the previous M Competition, at this address: `https://forecasters.org/resources/time-series-data/`.

One interesting aspect of the competition is that it dealt with consumer goods sales both fast-moving and slow-moving with many examples of the latest presenting intermittent sales (sales are often zero but for some rare cases). Intermittent series, though common in many industries, are still a challenging case in forecasting for many practitioners.

The competition timeline was arranged in two parts. In the first, from the beginning of March 2020 to June 1st, competitors could train models on the range of days up to day 1,913 and score their submission on the public test set (ranging from day 1,914 to 1,941). After that date, until the end of the competition on July 1st, the public test set was made available as part of the training set, allowing participants to tune their models in order to predict from day 1,942 to 1,969 (a time window of 28 days, i.e., four weeks). In that period, submissions were not scored on the leaderboard.

The rationale behind such an arrangement of the competition was to allow teams initially to test their models on the leaderboard and to have grounds to share their best-performing methods in notebooks and discussions. After the first phase, the organizers wanted to avoid having the leaderboard used for overfitting purposes or hyperparameter tuning of the models and they wanted to resemble a forecasting situation, as it would happen in the real world. In addition, the requirement to choose only one submission as the final one mirrored the same necessity for realism. In the real world, even if you adopt an MLOps champion/challenger strategy (see `https://www.datarobot.com/blog/introducing-mlops-champion-challenger-models/`), at a certain point, you have to decide what model to trust for your decisions and only afterward you get the outcome of your choice.

As for the data, we mentioned that the data was provided by Walmart and it represented the USA market: it originated from 10 stores in California, Wisconsin, and Texas. Specifically, the data was made up of the sales of 3,049 products, organized into 3 categories (hobbies, food, and household) that can be divided furthermore into 7 departments each. Such a hierarchical structure is certainly a challenge because you can model sale dynamics at the level of the USA market, state market, single store, product category, category department, and finally, specific product.

All these levels can also combine as different aggregates, which are something required to be predicted in the second track, the uncertainty track. The aggregates can be computed by the groupby method in pandas (see `https://www.kaggle.com/lucamassaron/m5-aggregations`), and they provide you with an idea of the complexity of the data you are working on as well as the different facets of the data that you can observe from a business point of view. Also, please notice how, as we get toward the product level, sales become sparse, with many items having days with very few or even no sales at all. Sparsity tends to prove difficult to handle for many traditional forecasting approaches:

Level ID	Level description	Aggregation level	Number of series
1	All products, aggregated for all stores and states	Total	1
2	All products, aggregated for each state	State	3
3	All products, aggregated for each store	Store	10
4	All products, aggregated for each category	Category	3
5	All products, aggregated for each department	Department	7
6	All products, aggregated for each state and category	State-Category	9
7	All products, aggregated for each state and department	State-Department	21
8	All products, aggregated for each store and category	Store-Category	30
9	All products, aggregated for each store and department	Store-Department	70
10	Each product, aggregated for all stores/states	Product	3,049
11	Each product, aggregated for each state	Product-State	9,147
12	Each product, aggregated for each store	Product-Store	30,490

From the point of view of time, the granularity is daily sales record and covered the period spanning from January 29th 2011 to June 19th 2016, which equals to 1,969 days in total: 1,913 for training, 28 for validation (public leaderboard), and 28 for testing (private leaderboard). A forecasting horizon of 28 days is actually recognized in the retail sector as the proper horizon for handling stocks and re-ordering operations for most goods.

Let's examine the different data you receive for the competition. You get sales_train_evaluation. csv, sell_prices.csv, and calendar.csv. The one keeping the time series is sales_train_ evaluation.csv. It is composed of fields that act as identifiers (item_id, dept_id, cat_id, store_ id, and state_id) and columns from d_1 to d_1941 representing the sales of those days:

	id	item_id	dept_id	cat_id	store_id	state_id	d_1	d_2	d_3	d_4	...	d_1932	d_1933	d_1934	d_1935	d_1936	d_1937	d_1938	d_1939	d_1940	d_1941
0	HOBBIES_1_001_CA_1_evaluation	HOBBIES_1_001	HOBBIES_1	HOBBIES	CA_1	CA	0	0	0	0	...	2	4	0	0	0	0	3	3	0	1
1	HOBBIES_1_002_CA_1_evaluation	HOBBIES_1_002	HOBBIES_1	HOBBIES	CA_1	CA	0	0	0	0	...	0	1	2	1	1	0	0	0	0	0
2	HOBBIES_1_003_CA_1_evaluation	HOBBIES_1_003	HOBBIES_1	HOBBIES	CA_1	CA	0	0	0	0	...	1	0	2	0	0	0	2	3	0	1
3	HOBBIES_1_004_CA_1_evaluation	HOBBIES_1_004	HOBBIES_1	HOBBIES	CA_1	CA	0	0	0	0	...	1	1	0	4	0	1	3	0	2	6
4	HOBBIES_1_005_CA_1_evaluation	HOBBIES_1_005	HOBBIES_1	HOBBIES	CA_1	CA	0	0	0	0	...	0	0	0	2	1	0	0	2	1	0

Figure 2.1: The sales_train_evaluation.csv data

`sell_prices.csv` contains information about the price of the items instead. The difficulty here is in joining the wm_yr_wk (the ID of the week) with the columns in the training data:

	store_id	item_id	wm_yr_wk	sell_price
0	CA_1	HOBBIES_1_001	11325	9.58
1	CA_1	HOBBIES_1_001	11326	9.58
2	CA_1	HOBBIES_1_001	11327	8.26
3	CA_1	HOBBIES_1_001	11328	8.26
4	CA_1	HOBBIES_1_001	11329	8.26

Figure 2.2: The sell_prices.csv data

The last file, `calendar.csv`, contains data relative to events that could have affected the sales:

	date	wm_yr_wk	weekday	wday	month	year	d	event_name_1	event_type_1	event_name_2	event_type_2	snap_CA	snap_TX	snap_WI
0	2011-01-29	11101	Saturday	1	1	2011	d_1	NaN	NaN	NaN	NaN	0	0	0
1	2011-01-30	11101	Sunday	2	1	2011	d_2	NaN	NaN	NaN	NaN	0	0	0
2	2011-01-31	11101	Monday	3	1	2011	d_3	NaN	NaN	NaN	NaN	0	0	0
3	2011-02-01	11101	Tuesday	4	2	2011	d_4	NaN	NaN	NaN	NaN	1	1	0
4	2011-02-02	11101	Wednesday	5	2	2011	d_5	NaN	NaN	NaN	NaN	1	0	1

Figure 2.3: The calendar.csv data

Again, the main challenge seems to join the data to the columns in the training table. Anyway, here you can get an easy key to connect columns (the d field) with the wm_yr_wk. In addition, in the table, we have represented different events that may have occurred on particular days as well as the **Supplement Nutrition Assistance Program (SNAP)** days, which are special days when the nutrition assistance benefits to help lower-income families can be used.

Understanding the Evaluation Metric

The accuracy competition introduced a new evaluation metric: **Weighted Root Mean Squared Scaled Error (WRMSSE)**. You first start from the RMSSE of individual time series under scrutiny. The metric evaluates the deviation of the point forecasts around the mean of the realized values of the series being predicted:

$$RMSSE = \sqrt{\frac{1}{h}\frac{\sum_{t=n+1}^{n+h}\left(Y_t - \widehat{Y}_t\right)^2}{\frac{1}{n-1}\sum_{t=2}^{n}(Y_t - Y_{t-1})^2}}$$

where:

- n is the length of the training sample
- h is the forecasting horizon (in our case, it is $h = 28$)
- Y_t is the sales value at time t; $\hat{Y}_t$ is the predicted value at time t

After estimating the RMSSE for all the 42,840 time series of the competition, the Weighted RMSSE will be computed as:

$$WRMSSE = \sum_{i=1}^{42,840} w_i * RMSSE$$

where w_i is the weight of the i_{th} series of the competition.

In the competition guidelines (`https://mofc.unic.ac.cy/m5-competition/`), in regard to RMSSE and WRMSSE, it is stated that:

- The denominator of RMSSE is computed only for the time periods for which the examined product(s) are actively sold, i.e., the periods following the first non-zero demand observed for the series under evaluation.
- The measure is scale independent, meaning that it can be effectively used to compare forecasts across series with different scales, thus you can compare the efficacy of the model across products at different sales quantities.
- In contrast to other measures, it can be safely computed as it does not rely on divisions with values that could be equal or close to zero (e.g., as done in percentage errors when $Y_t = 0$ or relative errors when the error of the benchmark used for scaling is zero).
- The measure penalizes positive and negative forecast errors, as well as large and small forecasts, equally, thus being symmetric.
- The weight of each series will be computed based on the last 28 observations of the training sample of the dataset, i.e., the cumulative actual dollar sales that each series displayed in that particular period (sum of units sold multiplied by their respective price).
- A lower WRMSSE is better.

A good explanation of the underlying workings of this is provided by this post from Alexander Soare (`https://www.kaggle.com/alexandersoare`): `https://www.kaggle.com/competitions/m5-forecasting-accuracy/discussion/137019`. After having transformed the evaluation metric, Alexander attributes better performances to improving the ratio between the error in the predictions and the day-to-day variation of sales values.

If the error is the same as the daily variations (ratio=1), it is likely that the model is not much better than a random guess based on historical variations. If your ratio is better than a random guess, it is converted into WRMSSE in a quadratic way (because of the square root in the formula). Consequently, a ratio of 0.7 corresponds to a WRMSSE of 0.5, and a ratio of 0.5 corresponds to a WRMSSE of 0.25.

During the competition, Kagglers just evaluated their models directly on the leaderboard but many attempts have also been made at using the metric directly as an objective function. First, the Tweedie loss (implemented both in XGBoost and LightGBM) worked quite well for the problem because it could handle the skewed distributions of sales for most products (a lot of them also had intermittent sales and that is also handled finely by the Tweedie loss). Here is the Tweedie loss formula:

$$Loss = -\sum_i x_i * \frac{\tilde{x}_i^{1-p}}{1-p} + \frac{\tilde{x}_i^{2-p}}{2-p}$$

In the formula, x_i represents the actual target; $\tilde{x}_i$ is the predicted value. You can find more information on the formula and its implementation in this article: `https://towardsdatascience.com/tweedie-loss-function-for-right-skewed-data-2c5ca470678f`.

The Poisson and Gamma distributions can be considered extreme cases of the Tweedie distribution: based on the parameter power, p, with p =1 you get a Poisson distribution, and with p =2, a Gamma one. Such a power parameter is actually the glue that keeps the mean and the variance of the distribution connected by the formula:

$$Var(x) = \Phi\mu^p$$

where Φ is the dispersion parameter and μ is the mean.

Using a power value between 1 and 2, you actually get a mix of Poisson and Gamma distributions, which can fit the competition problem very well. Most of the Kagglers involved in the competition using a GBM solution actually resorted to Tweedie loss.

In spite of Tweedie's success, some other Kagglers found interesting ways to implement an objective loss more similar to WRMSSE for their models:

- Martin Kovacevic Buvinic with his asymmetric loss: `https://www.kaggle.com/code/ragnar123/simple-lgbm-groupkfold-cv/notebook`
- Timetraveller using PyTorch Autograd to get gradient and hessian for any differentiable continuous loss function to be implemented in LightGBM: `https://www.kaggle.com/competitions/m5-forecasting-accuracy/discussion/152837`

Examining the 4th place solution's ideas from Monsaraida

There are many solutions available for the competition, mostly found on the competition Kaggle discussions pages. The top five methods of both challenges have also been gathered and published (except one because of proprietary rights) by the competition organizers themselves: https://github.com/Mcompetitions/M5-methods (by the way, reproducing the results of the winning submissions was a prerequisite for the collection of a competition prize).

Noticeably, all the Kagglers that placed in the higher ranks of the competitions have used, as their unique model type or in blended/stacked in ensembles, LightGBM because of its lesser memory usage and speed of computations, which gave it an advantage in the competition because of the large amount of times series to process and predict. But there are also other reasons for its success. Contrary to classical methods based on ARIMA, it doesn't require relying on the analysis of auto-correlation and specifically figuring out the parameters for every single series in the problem. In addition, distinguishing from methods based on deep learning, it doesn't require striving to improve complicated neural architectures or tuning a large number of hyperparameters. The strength of the gradient-boosting methods in time series problems (not only LightGBM but also, for instance, XGBoost) is based on feature engineering (based on time lags, moving averages, and averages from groupings of the series attributes), choosing the right objective function, and hyperparameters tuning. These methods are more effective than classical methods in the case of long enough time series. For shorter series, classical standard and linear statistical methods such as **auto-regressive (AR)**, **moving averages (MA)**, and **ARMA/ARIMA** are still the recommended choice since using more complex methods tends to overfit.

 Another advantage of LightGBM and XGBoost over deep learning solutions in the competition was the ready availability of Tweedie loss. In addition, other advantages over DNNs are not requiring any feature scaling (deep learning networks are particularly sensitive to the scaling you use) and the speed of training, which allowed faster iterations while testing feature engineering.

Among all these available solutions, we found the one proposed by Monsaraida (Masanori Miyahara), a Japanese computer scientist, the most interesting one. He proposed a simple and straightforward solution that has ranked fourth on the private leaderboard with a score of 0.53583. The solution uses just general features without prior selection (such as sales statistics, calendars, prices, and identifiers).

Moreover, it uses a limited number of models of the same kind, using LightGBM gradient boosting, without resorting to any kind of blending, recursive modeling when predictions feed other hierarchically related predictions or multipliers that are choosing constants to fit the test set better.

Here is a scheme taken from his solution presentation to M Forecasting Competitions (`https://github.com/Mcompetitions/M5-methods/tree/master/Code%20of%20Winning%20Methods/A4`), where we can note that he treats each of the ten stores by each of the four weeks to be looked at in the future, which, in the end, corresponds to producing 40 models:

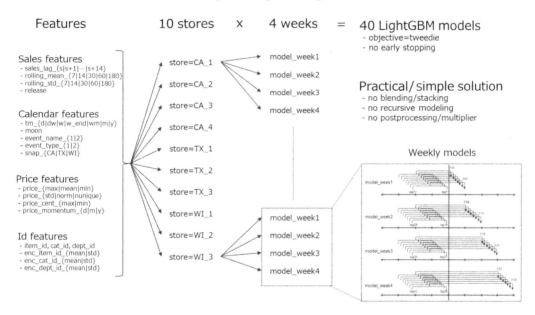

Figure 2.4: Explanation by Monsaraida of the structure of his solution

Masanori Miyahara

`https://www.kaggle.com/monsaraida`

Curious about his finely crafted solution and his Kaggle background, we contacted Masanori Miyahara (Monsaraida) who kindly replied to us and told us that he has a degree in computer science and that up to now, he has worked as a project leader in software development and data analysis projects for a Japanese company. He was initially interested in Kaggle because it would allow him to try various data techniques that he doesn't often use in his job.

What's your favorite kind of competition and why? In terms of techniques and solving approaches, what is your specialty on Kaggle?

I have participated in several image data and natural language processing competitions, but I participate most often in tabular data competitions. I think tabular data competitions are suitable for concentrating on for a short period because they are easy to participate in even if you don't have the computing resources, and you can finish one experiment quickly and do a lot of trial and error. (I am usually busy with childcare and work, so I tend to work on competitions in batches during vacations or on weekends.) Also, tabular data competitions can be fun even if you don't have advanced machine learning knowledge, as you can gradually improve your ranking by carefully exploring the data and trying original ideas based on your domain knowledge.

How do you approach a Kaggle competition? If you work in data science, how different is this approach to what you do in your day-to-day work?

For me, participating in a Kaggle competition is similar to buying and playing a video game or going on a trip; it is a complete hobby. If I am interested in a dataset or problem, I make some alone time during vacation or at weekends to work on a competition. I generally enter competitions solo. This is because I do not want to inconvenience my team members by being unable to devote time to competitions due to childcare or work. On the other hand, in business, we work systematically as a team to understand and solve customers' problems. The most important thing is providing customer value, and there are few opportunities to take a prediction model's accuracy to the extreme. Reproducibility, stability, maintainability, and cost performance are also necessary for business. In Kaggle, everything should be worked on to improve accuracy by even just 0.1%, and factors other than accuracy are often less critical.

Has Kaggle helped you in your career? If so, how?

Kaggle is a hobby for me, so I am not working on it because I think it will help my career. However, as a result, it is useful for my career. Recently, Kaggle has become very popular in Japan and many people are interested in it. When I tell people that I am working on competitions in Kaggle, they trust me and often ask me for advice on data analysis. I have also learned a lot from Kaggle about validation strategies that prevent overfitting and guarantee accuracy in a real-world environment, and it has been very useful in my work. A wrong validation strategy in business can be very damaging, but in Kaggle, I can only miss out on a medal. Furthermore, the Kaggle experience has allowed me to estimate how much time I need to spend to improve the accuracy after only a short checking of the data.

In your experience, what do inexperienced Kagglers often overlook? What do you know now that you wish you'd known when you first started?

This is my personal opinion, but I believe that when learning something, it is much more efficient to work on something you love, something you can lose track of time and become passionate about. I am sometimes asked the question, "Should I study Python or read a machine learning textbook to gain enough knowledge before working on the Kaggle competition?" I think you should participate in the current competition anyway. When you participate in a competition and submit your predictions, you will know where you rank and will want to improve your ranking. To improve your ranking, you will need coding skills and knowledge of machine learning and data analysis, and you should start studying the knowledge required to do so. Since you have a clear objective, you can learn efficiently, and the results of what you learn will be immediately reflected in your rankings, which will motivate you.

Are there any particular tools or libraries that you would recommend using for data analysis/machine learning?

Of course, data analysis and machine learning libraries such as pandas/scikit-learn/LightGBM/XG-Boost are recommended, but I think experiment management tools such as MLflow are also essential for efficient experiments. If you repeatedly perform trial-and-error experiments without an experiment management tool, you will lose track of the experimental conditions and settings. You can conduct experiments efficiently by ensuring reproducibility with an experiment management tool, especially in the latter half of the competition.

What's the most important thing someone should keep in mind/do when they're entering a competition?

I think the most important thing is to enjoy Kaggle. There are many ways to enjoy Kaggle: enjoy the competition, enjoy the new data and domain knowledge, enjoy the latest techniques and tools, enjoy the discussions with others, etc. Whatever the outcome, the time spent having fun and the knowledge gained is very worthwhile.

Given that Monsaraida has kept his solution simple and practical, like in a real-world forecasting project, in this chapter, we will try to replicate his example by refactoring his code in order to run in Kaggle notebooks (we will handle the memory and the running time limitations by splitting the code into multiple notebooks). In this way, we intend to provide the readers with a simple and effective way, based on gradient boosting, to approach forecasting problems.

Computing predictions for specific dates and time horizons

The plan for replicating Monsaraida's solution is to create a notebook customizable by input parameters to produce the necessary processed data for training and test datasets and the LightGBM models for predictions. The models, given data in the past, will be trained to learn to predict values in a specific number of days in the future. The best results can be obtained by having each model learn to predict the values in a specific week range in the future. Since we have to predict up to 28 days ahead, we need a model predicting from day +1 to day +7 in the future, then another one able to predict from day +8 to day +14, another from day +15 to +21, and finally, another one capable of handling predictions from day +22 to day +28. We will need a Kaggle notebook for each of these time ranges, thus we need four notebooks. Each of these notebooks will be trained to predict the future time span for each of the 10 stores that were part of the competition. In total, each notebook will produce ten models. Altogether, the notebooks will then produce 40 models covering all the future ranges and all the stores.

Since we need to predict both for the public leaderboard and for the private one, it is necessary to repeat this process twice, stopping training at day 1,913 (predicting days from 1,914 to 1,941) for the public test set submission, and at day 1,941 (predicting days from 1,942 to 1,969) for the private one.

Given the current limitations for running Kaggle notebooks based on CPU, all these eight notebooks can be run in parallel (the whole process takes almost 6 and a half hours). Each notebook can be distinguishable by others by its name, containing the parameters' values relative to the last training day and the look-ahead horizon in days. An example of one of these notebooks can be found at `https://www.kaggle.com/code/lucamassaron/m5-train-day-1941-horizon-7`.

Using all the stores and all the items when experimenting and testing feature engineering in this competition can take up a lot of computing time. We suggest using a single store or a single state to reduce the number of rows in the dataset. Slicing the data in this way will allow the machine learning algorithm to deal with much less information (and to be much speedier for faster experimentation iterations) without losing important correlations that may exist between categories, clusters of items, or even between couples of single items.

Let's now examine together how the code has been arranged and what we can learn from Monsaraida's solution.

We simply start by importing the necessary packages. You can just notice how, apart from NumPy and pandas, the only data science specialized package is LightGBM. You may also notice that we are going to use gc (garbage collection): that's because we need to limit the amount of memory used by the script, and we frequently just collect and recycle the unused memory.

As part of this strategy, we also frequently store models and data structures on disk, instead of keeping them in memory:

```python
import numpy as np
import pandas as pd
import os
import random
import math
from decimal import Decimal as dec
import datetime
import time
import gc
import lightgbm as lgb
import pickle

import warnings
warnings.filterwarnings("ignore", category=UserWarning)
```

As part of the strategy to limit memory usage, we resort to the function to reduce the pandas DataFrame memory footprint, described in the Kaggle book and initially developed by Arjan Groen during the Zillow competition (read the discussion at https://www.kaggle.com/competitions/ tabular-playground-series-dec-2021/discussion/291844):

```python
def reduce_mem_usage(df, verbose=True):
    numerics = ['int16', 'int32', 'int64', 'float16', 'float32',
'float64']
    start_mem = df.memory_usage().sum() / 1024**2
    for col in df.columns:
        col_type = df[col].dtypes
        if col_type in numerics:
            c_min = df[col].min()
            c_max = df[col].max()
            if str(col_type)[:3] == 'int':
                if c_min > np.iinfo(np.int8).min and c_max < np.
int8).max:
                    df[col] = df[col].astype(np.int8)
                elif c_min > np.iinfo(np.int16).min and c_max <
np.iinfo(np.int16).max:
                    df[col] = df[col].astype(np.int16)
                elif c_min > np.iinfo(np.int32).min and c_max <
np.iinfo(np.int32).max:
                    df[col] = df[col].astype(np.int32)
```

```
            elif c_min > np.iinfo(np.int64).min and c_max <
np.iinfo(np.int64).max:
                    df[col] = df[col].astype(np.int64)
        else:
                if c_min > np.finfo(np.float32).min and c_max <
np.finfo(np.float32).max:
                    df[col] = df[col].astype(np.float32)
            else:
                    df[col] = df[col].astype(np.float64)
    end_mem = df.memory_usage().sum() / 1024**2
    if verbose: print('Mem. usage decreased to {:5.2f} Mb ({:.1f}%
reduction)'.format(end_mem, 100 * (start_mem - end_mem) / start_mem))
    return df
```

We keep on defining functions for this solution, because splitting the solution into smaller parts helps and because it is easier to clean up all the used variables when you just return from a function (you keep only what you saved to disk). Our next function helps us to load all the data available and compress it:

```
def load_data():
    train_df = reduce_mem_usage(pd.read_csv("../input/m5-forecasting-
accuracy/sales_train_evaluation.csv"))
    prices_df = reduce_mem_usage(pd.read_csv("../input/m5-forecasting-
accuracy/sell_prices.csv"))
    calendar_df = reduce_mem_usage(pd.read_csv("../input/m5-forecasting-
accuracy/calendar.csv"))
    submission_df = reduce_mem_usage(pd.read_csv("../input/m5-forecasting-
accuracy/sample_submission.csv"))
    return train_df, prices_df, calendar_df, submission_df
```

Once the function has been defined, we run it:

```
train_df, prices_df, calendar_df, submission_df = load_data()
```

After preparing the code to retrieve the data relative to prices, volumes, and calendar information, we proceed to prepare the first processing function that will have the role to create a basic table of information having `item_id`, `dept_id`, `cat_id`, `state_id`, and `store_id` as row keys, a day column, and a values column containing the volumes. This is achieved starting from rows having all the days' data columns by using the pandas command `melt` (`https://pandas.pydata.org/pandas-docs/stable/reference/api/pandas.melt.html`).

The command takes as reference the index of the DataFrame and then picks all the remaining features, placing their name on a column and their value on another one (var_name and value_ name parameters help you define the name of these new columns). In this way, you can unfold a row representing the sales series of a certain item in a certain store into multiple rows, each one representing a single day. The fact that the positional order of the unfolded columns is preserved guarantees that now your time series spans on the vertical axis (you can therefore apply further-more transformations on it, such as moving means).

To give you an idea of what is happening, here is the train_df before the transformation with pd.melt. Notice how the volumes of the distinct days are column features:

```
train_df.head()
```

	id	item_id	dept_id	cat_id	store_id	state_id	d_1	d_2	d_3	d_4	...	d_1932	d_1933	d_1934	d_1935	d_1936	d_1937	d_1938	d_1939	d_1940	d_1941
0	HOBBIES_1_001_CA_1_evaluation	HOBBIES_1_001	HOBBIES_1	HOBBIES	CA_1	CA	0	0	0	0	...	2	4	0	0	0	0	3	3	0	1
1	HOBBIES_1_002_CA_1_evaluation	HOBBIES_1_002	HOBBIES_1	HOBBIES	CA_1	CA	0	0	0	0	...	0	1	2	1	1	0	0	0	0	0
2	HOBBIES_1_003_CA_1_evaluation	HOBBIES_1_003	HOBBIES_1	HOBBIES	CA_1	CA	0	0	0	0	...	1	0	2	0	0	0	2	3	0	1
3	HOBBIES_1_004_CA_1_evaluation	HOBBIES_1_004	HOBBIES_1	HOBBIES	CA_1	CA	0	0	0	0	...	1	1	0	4	0	1	3	0	2	6
4	HOBBIES_1_005_CA_1_evaluation	HOBBIES_1_005	HOBBIES_1	HOBBIES	CA_1	CA	0	0	0	0	...	0	0	0	2	1	0	0	2	1	0

5 rows × 1947 columns

Figure 2.5: The training DataFrame

After the transformation, you obtain a grid_df, where the columns have been converted into rows, and days are now to be found under a new column:

```
grid_df.head()
```

	id	item_id	dept_id	cat_id	store_id	state_id	d	sales	release
0	HOBBIES_1_001_CA_1_evaluation	HOBBIES_1_001	HOBBIES_1	HOBBIES	CA_1	CA	1	0.0	224
1	HOBBIES_1_002_CA_1_evaluation	HOBBIES_1_002	HOBBIES_1	HOBBIES	CA_1	CA	1	0.0	20
2	HOBBIES_1_003_CA_1_evaluation	HOBBIES_1_003	HOBBIES_1	HOBBIES	CA_1	CA	1	0.0	300
3	HOBBIES_1_004_CA_1_evaluation	HOBBIES_1_004	HOBBIES_1	HOBBIES	CA_1	CA	1	0.0	5
4	HOBBIES_1_005_CA_1_evaluation	HOBBIES_1_005	HOBBIES_1	HOBBIES	CA_1	CA	1	0.0	16

Figure 2.6: Applying pd.melt to the training DataFrame

The feature d contains the reference to the columns that are not part of the index, in essence, all the features from d_1 to d_1935. This implies an increase of the number of rows in the dataset by 1,935 fold. By simply removing the d_ prefix from its values and converting them to integers, you now have a day feature.

Apart from this, the code snippet also separates a holdout of the rows. Such a holdout is your validation set. The validation strategy is based on reserving a part of the training data, based on time. On the training part, it will also add the rows necessary for your predictions based on the prediction horizon (the number of days you want to predict in the future) you provide.

Here is the function that creates our basic feature template. As input, it takes the train_df Data-Frame, the number of the day the training ends, and the prediction horizon:

```
def generate_base_grid(train_df, end_train_day_x, predict_horizon):
    index_columns = ['id', 'item_id', 'dept_id', 'cat_id', 'store_id',
 'state_id']

    grid_df = pd.melt(train_df, id_vars=index_columns, var_name='d',
 value_name='sales')
    grid_df = reduce_mem_usage(grid_df, verbose=False)

    grid_df['d_org'] = grid_df['d']
    grid_df['d'] = grid_df['d'].apply(lambda x: x[2:]).astype(np.int16)

    time_mask = (grid_df['d'] > end_train_day_x) &  (grid_df['d'] <= end_
train_day_x + predict_horizon)
    holdout_df = grid_df.loc[time_mask, ["id", "d", "sales"]].reset_
index(drop=True)
    holdout_df.to_feather(f"holdout_df_{end_train_day_x}_to_{end_train_
day_x + predict_horizon}.feather")
    del(holdout_df)
    gc.collect()

    grid_df = grid_df[grid_df['d'] <= end_train_day_x]
    grid_df['d'] = grid_df['d_org']
    grid_df = grid_df.drop('d_org', axis=1)

    add_grid = pd.DataFrame()
    for i in range(predict_horizon):
        temp_df = train_df[index_columns]
        temp_df = temp_df.drop_duplicates()
        temp_df['d'] = 'd_' + str(end_train_day_x + i + 1)
        temp_df['sales'] = np.nan
        add_grid = pd.concat([add_grid, temp_df])
```

```
    grid_df = pd.concat([grid_df, add_grid])
    grid_df = grid_df.reset_index(drop=True)

    for col in index_columns:
        grid_df[col] = grid_df[col].astype('category')

    grid_df = reduce_mem_usage(grid_df, verbose=False)
    grid_df.to_feather(f"grid_df_{end_train_day_x}_to_{end_train_day_x +
predict_horizon}.feather")
    del(grid_df)
    gc.collect()
```

After handling the function to create the basic feature template, we prepare a merge function for pandas DataFrames that will help to save memory space and avoid memory errors when handling large sets of data. Given two DataFrames, df1 and df2, and the set of foreign keys we need to be merged, the function applies a left outer join between df1 and df2 without creating a new merged object but simply expands the existent df1 DataFrame.

The function works first by extracting the foreign keys from df1, then merging the extracted keys with df2. In this way, the function creates a new DataFrame, called merged_gf, which is ordered as df1. At this point, we just assign the merged_gf columns to df1. Internally, df1 will pick the reference to the internal data structures from merged_gf. Such an approach helps minimize memory usage because only the necessary used data is created at any time (there are no duplicates that can fill up the memory). When the function returns df1, merged_gf is canceled except for the data now used by df1.

Here is the code for this utility function:

```
def merge_by_concat(df1, df2, merge_on):
    merged_gf = df1[merge_on]
    merged_gf = merged_gf.merge(df2, on=merge_on, how='left')
    new_columns = [col for col in list(merged_gf)
                    if col not in merge_on]
    df1[new_columns] = merged_gf[new_columns]
    return df1
```

After this necessary step, we proceed to program a new function to process the data. This time, we handle the prices data, a set of data containing the prices of each item by each store for all the weeks. Since it is important to figure out if we are talking about a new product appearing in a store or not, the function picks the first date of price availability (using the wm_yr_wk feature in the price table, representing the ID of the week) and it copies it to our feature template.

Here is the code for processing the release dates:

```
def calc_release_week(prices_df, end_train_day_x, predict_horizon):
    index_columns = ['id', 'item_id', 'dept_id', 'cat_id', 'store_id',
'state_id']

    grid_df = pd.read_feather(f"grid_df_{end_train_day_x}_to_{end_train_
day_x + predict_horizon}.feather")

    release_df = prices_df.groupby(['store_id', 'item_id'])['wm_yr_wk'].
agg(['min']).reset_index()
    release_df.columns = ['store_id', 'item_id', 'release']

    grid_df = merge_by_concat(grid_df, release_df, ['store_id', 'item_
id'])

    del release_df
    grid_df = reduce_mem_usage(grid_df, verbose=False)
    gc.collect()

    grid_df = merge_by_concat(grid_df, calendar_df[['wm_yr_wk', 'd']],
['d'])
```

```
    grid_df = grid_df.reset_index(drop=True)

    grid_df['release'] = grid_df['release'] - grid_df['release'].min()
    grid_df['release'] = grid_df['release'].astype(np.int16)

    grid_df = reduce_mem_usage(grid_df, verbose=False)
    grid_df.to_feather(f"grid_df_{end_train_day_x}_to_{end_train_day_x +
  predict_horizon}.feather")
    del(grid_df)
    gc.collect()
```

After having handled the day of the product appearance in a store, we proceed to deal with the prices. In regard to each item, by each shop, we prepare basic price features showing:

- The actual price (normalized by the maximum)
- The maximum price
- The minimum price
- The mean price
- The standard deviation of the price
- The number of different prices the item has taken
- The number of items in the store with the same price

Besides these basic descriptive statistics of prices, we also add some features to describe their dynamics for each item in a store based on different time granularities:

- The day momentum, i.e., the ratio before the actual price and its price the previous day
- The month momentum, i.e., the ratio before the actual price and its average price the same month
- The year momentum, i.e., the ratio before the actual price and its average price the same year

Exercise 1

Can you build more price-based features? For instance, by using other descriptive statistics than mean and variance or processing other time granularity (for instance, week or quarterly based)?

Exercise Notes (write down any notes or workings that will help you):

Here we use two interesting and essential pandas methods for time series feature processing:

- `shift`: This can move the index forward or backward by n steps (`https://pandas.pydata.org/pandas-docs/stable/reference/api/pandas.DataFrame.shift.html`)

- `transform`: This, applied to each group, fills a same-index feature with the transformed values (`https://pandas.pydata.org/docs/reference/api/pandas.core.groupby.DataFrameGroupBy.transform.html`)

In addition, the decimal part of the price is processed as a feature, in order to reveal a situation when the item is sold at psychological pricing thresholds (e.g., $19.99 or £2.98 – see this discussion: `https://www.kaggle.com/competitions/m5-forecasting-accuracy/discussion/145011`).

The function `math.modf` (`https://docs.python.org/3.8/library/math.html#math.modf`) helps in doing so because it splits any floating-point number into fractional and integer parts (a two-item tuple).

Finally, the resulting table is saved onto disk.

Here is the function doing all the feature engineering on prices:

```
def generate_grid_price(prices_df, calendar_df, end_train_day_x, predict_
horizon):

    grid_df = pd.read_feather(f"grid_df_{end_train_day_x}_to_{end_train_
day_x + predict_horizon}.feather")

    prices_df['price_max'] = prices_df.groupby(['store_id', 'item_id'])
['sell_price'].transform('max')
    prices_df['price_min'] = prices_df.groupby(['store_id', 'item_id'])
['sell_price'].transform('min')
    prices_df['price_std'] = prices_df.groupby(['store_id', 'item_id'])
['sell_price'].transform('std')
    prices_df['price_mean'] = prices_df.groupby(['store_id', 'item_id'])
['sell_price'].transform('mean')
    prices_df['price_norm'] = prices_df['sell_price'] / prices_df['price_
max']
    prices_df['price_nunique'] = prices_df.groupby(['store_id', 'item_
id'])['sell_price'].transform('nunique')
    prices_df['item_nunique'] = prices_df.groupby(['store_id', 'sell_
price'])['item_id'].transform('nunique')
```

```
    calendar_prices = calendar_df[['wm_yr_wk', 'month', 'year']]
    calendar_prices = calendar_prices.drop_duplicates(subset=['wm_yr_wk'])
    prices_df = prices_df.merge(calendar_prices[['wm_yr_wk', 'month',
'year']], on=['wm_yr_wk'], how='left')

    del calendar_prices
    gc.collect()

    prices_df['price_momentum'] = prices_df['sell_price'] / prices_
df.groupby(['store_id', 'item_id'])[
        'sell_price'].transform(lambda x: x.shift(1))
    prices_df['price_momentum_m'] = prices_df['sell_price'] / prices_
df.groupby(['store_id', 'item_id', 'month'])[
        'sell_price'].transform('mean')
    prices_df['price_momentum_y'] = prices_df['sell_price'] / prices_
df.groupby(['store_id', 'item_id', 'year'])[
        'sell_price'].transform('mean')

    prices_df['sell_price_cent'] = [math.modf(p)[0] for p in prices_
df['sell_price']]
    prices_df['price_max_cent'] = [math.modf(p)[0] for p in prices_
df['price_max']]
    prices_df['price_min_cent'] = [math.modf(p)[0] for p in prices_
df['price_min']]

    del prices_df['month'], prices_df['year']
    prices_df = reduce_mem_usage(prices_df, verbose=False)
    gc.collect()

    original_columns = list(grid_df)
    grid_df = grid_df.merge(prices_df, on=['store_id', 'item_id', 'wm_yr_
wk'], how='left')
    del(prices_df)
    gc.collect()

    keep_columns = [col for col in list(grid_df) if col not in original_
columns]
```

```
      grid_df = grid_df[['id', 'd'] + keep_columns]
      grid_df = reduce_mem_usage(grid_df, verbose=False)

      grid_df.to_feather(f"grid_price_{end_train_day_x}_to_{end_train_day_x
  + predict_horizon}.feather")
      del(grid_df)
      gc.collect()
```

The next function computes the moon phase, returning one of its eight phases (from new moon to waning crescent). Although moon phases shouldn't directly influence any sales (weather conditions instead do, but we have no weather information in the data), they represent a periodic cycle of 29 and a half days, which can well suit periodic shopping behaviors.

There is an interesting discussion, with different hypotheses regarding why moon phases may work as a predictor, in this competition post: `https://www.kaggle.com/competitions/m5-forecasting-accuracy/discussion/154776`:

```
  def get_moon_phase(d):   # 0=new, 4=full; 4 days/phase
      diff = datetime.datetime.strptime(d, '%Y-%m-%d') - datetime.
  datetime(2001, 1, 1)
      days = dec(diff.days) + (dec(diff.seconds) / dec(86400))
      lunations = dec("0.20439731") + (days * dec("0.03386319269"))
      phase_index = math.floor((lunations % dec(1) * dec(8)) + dec('0.5'))
      return int(phase_index) & 7
```

The moon phase function is part of a general function for creating time-based features. The function takes the calendar dataset information and places it among the features. Such information contains events and their type as well as an indication of the SNAP periods that could drive furthermore sales of basic goods. The function also generates numeric features such as the day, the month, the year, the day of the week, the week in the month, and if it is the end of the week. Here is the code:

```
  def generate_grid_calendar(calendar_df, end_train_day_x, predict_horizon):

      grid_df = pd.read_feather(
                f"grid_df_{end_train_day_x}_to_{end_train_day_x +
                predict_horizon}.feather")

      grid_df = grid_df[['id', 'd']]
```

```
    gc.collect()

    calendar_df['moon'] = calendar_df.date.apply(get_moon_phase)

    # Merge calendar partly
    icols = ['date',
             'd',
             'event_name_1',
             'event_type_1',
             'event_name_2',
             'event_type_2',
             'snap_CA',
             'snap_TX',
             'snap_WI',
             'moon',
             ]

    grid_df = grid_df.merge(calendar_df[icols], on=['d'], how='left')

    icols = ['event_name_1',
             'event_type_1',
             'event_name_2',
             'event_type_2',
             'snap_CA',
             'snap_TX',
             'snap_WI']

    for col in icols:
        grid_df[col] = grid_df[col].astype('category')

    grid_df['date'] = pd.to_datetime(grid_df['date'])

    grid_df['tm_d'] = grid_df['date'].dt.day.astype(np.int8)
    grid_df['tm_w'] = grid_df['date'].dt.isocalendar().week.astype(np.
int8)
    grid_df['tm_m'] = grid_df['date'].dt.month.astype(np.int8)
    grid_df['tm_y'] = grid_df['date'].dt.year
```

```
    grid_df['tm_y'] = (grid_df['tm_y'] - grid_df['tm_y'].min()).astype(np.
int8)
    grid_df['tm_wm'] = grid_df['tm_d'].apply(lambda x: math.ceil(x / 7)).
astype(np.int8)

    grid_df['tm_dw'] = grid_df['date'].dt.dayofweek.astype(np.int8)
    grid_df['tm_w_end'] = (grid_df['tm_dw'] >= 5).astype(np.int8)

    del(grid_df['date'])
    grid_df = reduce_mem_usage(grid_df, verbose=False)
    grid_df.to_feather(f"grid_calendar_{end_train_day_x}_to_{end_train_
day_x + predict_horizon}.feather")

    del(grid_df)
    del(calendar_df)
    gc.collect()
```

The following function instead just removes the wm_yr_wk feature and transforms the d (day) feature into a numeric one. It is a necessary step for the feature transformation functions:

```
def modify_grid_base(end_train_day_x, predict_horizon):
    grid_df = pd.read_feather(f"grid_df_{end_train_day_x}_to_{end_train_
day_x + predict_horizon}.feather")
    grid_df['d'] = grid_df['d'].apply(lambda x: x[2:]).astype(np.int16)
    del grid_df['wm_yr_wk']

    grid_df = reduce_mem_usage(grid_df, verbose=False)
    grid_df.to_feather(f"grid_df_{end_train_day_x}_to_{end_train_day_x +
predict_horizon}.feather")

    del(grid_df)
    gc.collect()
```

Our last two feature creation functions will generate more sophisticated feature engineering for time series. The first function will produce both lagged sales and their moving averages. First, using the shift method will generate a range of lagged sales up to 15 days in the past. Then, using shift in conjunction with rolling (https://pandas.pydata.org/docs/reference/api/pandas.DataFrame.rolling.html) will create moving means with windows of 7, 14, 30, 60, and 180 days.

The `shift` command is necessary because it will allow moving the index so that you will always consider available data for your calculations. Hence, if your prediction horizon goes up to seven days, the calculations will consider only the data available seven days before. Then, the rolling command will create a moving window of observations that can be summarized (in this case by the mean). Having a mean over a period (the moving window) and following its evolutions will help you to detect better any changes in trends because patterns not repeating across the time windows will be leveled off. This is a common strategy in time series analysis to remove noise and non-interesting patterns. For instance, with a rolling mean of seven days, you will cancel all the daily patterns and just represent what happens to your sales on a weekly basis.

Exercise 2

Can you experiment with different moving average windows? Also trying different strategies may help. For instance, by exploring the Tabular Playground of January 2022 (`https://www.kaggle.com/competitions/tabular-playground-series-jan-2022`) devoted to time series, you may find more ideas since most solutions are built using gradient boosting.

Exercise Notes (write down any notes or workings that will help you):

Here is the code to generate the lag and rolling mean features:

```
def generate_lag_feature(end_train_day_x, predict_horizon):
    grid_df = pd.read_feather(f"grid_df_{end_train_day_x}_to_{end_train_
day_x + predict_horizon}.feather")
    grid_df = grid_df[['id', 'd', 'sales']]


    num_lag_day_list = []
    num_lag_day = 15
    for col in range(predict_horizon, predict_horizon + num_lag_day):
        num_lag_day_list.append(col)


    grid_df = grid_df.assign(**{
        '{}_lag_{}'.format(col, l): grid_df.groupby(['id'])['sales'].
transform(lambda x: x.shift(l))
        for l in num_lag_day_list
    })


    for col in list(grid_df):
        if 'lag' in col:
            grid_df[col] = grid_df[col].astype(np.float16)


    num_rolling_day_list = [7, 14, 30, 60, 180]
    for num_rolling_day in num_rolling_day_list:
        grid_df['rolling_mean_' + str(num_rolling_day)] = grid_
df.groupby(['id'])['sales'].transform(
            lambda x: x.shift(predict_horizon).rolling(num_rolling_day).
mean()).astype(np.float16)
        grid_df['rolling_std_' + str(num_rolling_day)] = grid_
df.groupby(['id'])['sales'].transform(
            lambda x: x.shift(predict_horizon).rolling(num_rolling_day).
std()).astype(np.float16)


    grid_df = reduce_mem_usage(grid_df, verbose=False)
    grid_df.to_feather(f"lag_feature_{end_train_day_x}_to_{end_train_day_x
+ predict_horizon}.feather")


    del(grid_df)
    gc.collect()
```

The second advanced feature engineering function is an encoding function, taking specific groupings of variables among state, store, category, department, and sold item and representing their mean and standard deviation. Such embeddings are time-independent (time is not part of the grouping) and they have the role of helping the training algorithm to distinguish how items, categories, and stores (and their combinations) differentiate among themselves.

Exercise 3

The proposed embeddings could also be computed using target encoding, as described in *The Kaggle Book* on page 216. Can you apply the target encoding embeddings and figure out how to obtain better results?

Exercise Notes (write down any notes or workings that will help you):

The code works by grouping the features, computing their descriptive statistic (the mean or the standard deviation in our case), and then applying the results to the dataset using the transform method that we discussed before:

```
def generate_target_encoding_feature(end_train_day_x, predict_horizon):

    grid_df = pd.read_feather(f"grid_df_{end_train_day_x}_to_{end_train_
day_x + predict_horizon}.feather")

    grid_df.loc[grid_df['d'] > (end_train_day_x - predict_horizon),
'sales'] = np.nan
    base_cols = list(grid_df)

    icols = [
        ['state_id'],
        ['store_id'],
        ['cat_id'],
        ['dept_id'],
        ['state_id', 'cat_id'],
        ['state_id', 'dept_id'],
        ['store_id', 'cat_id'],
        ['store_id', 'dept_id'],
        ['item_id'],
        ['item_id', 'state_id'],
        ['item_id', 'store_id']
    ]

    for col in icols:
        col_name = '_' + '_'.join(col) + '_'
        grid_df['enc' + col_name + 'mean'] = grid_df.groupby(col)
['sales'].transform('mean').astype(
            np.float16)
        grid_df['enc' + col_name + 'std'] = grid_df.groupby(col)['sales'].
transform('std').astype(
            np.float16)

    keep_cols = [col for col in list(grid_df) if col not in base_cols]
    grid_df = grid_df[['id', 'd'] + keep_cols]
```

```
    grid_df = reduce_mem_usage(grid_df, verbose=False)
    grid_df.to_feather(f"target_encoding_{end_train_day_x}_to_{end_train_
day_x + predict_horizon}.feather")

    del(grid_df)
    gc.collect()
```

Having completed the feature engineering part, we now proceed to put together all the files we have stored away on disk while generating the features. The following function just loads the different datasets of basic features, price features, calendar features, lag/rolling, and embedded features, and concatenates them all together. The code then filters only the rows relative to a specific shop to be saved as a separate dataset.

Such an approach matches the strategy of having a model trained on a specific store aimed at predicting for a specific time interval:

```
def assemble_grid_by_store(train_df, end_train_day_x, predict_horizon):
    grid_df = pd.concat([pd.read_feather(f"grid_df_{end_train_day_x}_to_
{end_train_day_x + predict_horizon}.feather"),
                    pd.read_feather(f"grid_price_{end_train_day_x}_to_
{end_train_day_x + predict_horizon}.feather").iloc[:, 2:],
                    pd.read_feather(f"grid_calendar_{end_train_day_x}_to_
{end_train_day_x + predict_horizon}.feather").iloc[:, 2:]],
                    axis=1)
    gc.collect()
    store_id_set_list = list(train_df['store_id'].unique())

    index_store = dict()
    for store_id in store_id_set_list:
        extract = grid_df[grid_df['store_id'] == store_id]
        index_store[store_id] = extract.index.to_numpy()
        extract = extract.reset_index(drop=True)
        extract.to_feather(f"grid_full_store_{store_id}_{end_train_day_x}_
to_{end_train_day_x + predict_horizon}.feather")

    del(grid_df)
    gc.collect()
```

```
    mean_features = [
        'enc_cat_id_mean', 'enc_cat_id_std',
        'enc_dept_id_mean', 'enc_dept_id_std',
        'enc_item_id_mean', 'enc_item_id_std'
        ]
    df2 = pd.read_feather(f"target_encoding_{end_train_day_x}_to_{end_
train_day_x + predict_horizon}.feather")[mean_features]


    for store_id in store_id_set_list:
        df = pd.read_feather(f"grid_full_store_{store_id}_{end_train_
day_x}_to_{end_train_day_x + predict_horizon}.feather")
        df = pd.concat([df, df2[df2.index.isin(index_store[store_id])].
reset_index(drop=True)], axis=1)
        df.to_feather(f"grid_full_store_{store_id}_{end_train_day_x}_to_
{end_train_day_x + predict_horizon}.feather")


    del(df2)
    gc.collect()


    df3 = pd.read_feather(f"lag_feature_{end_train_day_x}_to_{end_train_
day_x + predict_horizon}.feather").iloc[:, 3:]


    for store_id in store_id_set_list:
        df = pd.read_feather(f"grid_full_store_{store_id}_{end_train_
day_x}_to_{end_train_day_x + predict_horizon}.feather")
        df = pd.concat([df, df3[df3.index.isin(index_store[store_id])].
reset_index(drop=True)], axis=1)
        df.to_feather(f"grid_full_store_{store_id}_{end_train_day_x}_to_
{end_train_day_x + predict_horizon}.feather")


    del(df3)
    del(store_id_set_list)
    gc.collect()
```

The following function, instead, just further processes the selection from the previous one by removing unused features and reordering the columns, and it returns the data for a model to be trained on:

```
def load_grid_by_store(end_train_day_x, predict_horizon, store_id):
```

```
    df = pd.read_feather(f"grid_full_store_{store_id}_{end_train_day_x}_
to_{end_train_day_x + predict_horizon}.feather")


    remove_features = ['id', 'state_id', 'store_id', 'date', 'wm_yr_wk',
'd', 'sales']
    enable_features = [col for col in list(df) if col not in remove_
features]
    df = df[['id', 'd', 'sales'] + enable_features]
    df = reduce_mem_usage(df, verbose=False)
    gc.collect()


    return df, enable_features
```

Finally, we can now deal with the training phase. The following code snippet starts by defining the training parameters as explicated by Monsaraida being the most effective on the problem. For training time reasons, we just modified the boosting type, choosing to use **Gradient-Based One-Side Sampling (GOSS)** instead of **Gradient Boosting Decision Tree (GBDT)** because that can really speed up training without much loss in terms of performance. A good speed-up to the model is also provided by the subsample parameter and the feature fraction: at each learning step of the gradient boosting, only half of the examples and half of the features will be considered.

 Also compiling LightGBM on your machine with the right compiling options may increase your speed, as explained in this interesting competition discussion: https://www.kaggle.com/competitions/m5-forecasting-accuracy/discussion/148273

The Tweedie loss, with a power value of 1.1 (hence with an underlying distribution closer to Poisson) seems particularly effective in modeling intermittent series (where zero sales prevail). The used metric is just the root mean squared error (there is no necessity to use a custom metric for representing the competition metric). We also use the force_row_wise parameter to save memory in the Kaggle notebook. All the other parameters are exactly the ones presented by Monsaraida in his solution (apart from the subsampling parameter that has been disabled because of its incompatibility with the goss boosting type).

Exercise 4

In what other Kaggle competition has the Tweedie loss proven useful? Can you find useful discussions about this loss and its usage in Meta Kaggle by exploring the `ForumTopics` and `ForumMessages` CSV tables in the Meta Kaggle dataset (`https://www.kaggle.com/datasets/kaggle/meta-kaggle`)?

Exercise Notes (write down any notes or workings that will help you):

After defining the training parameters, we just iterate over the stores, each time uploading the training data of a single store and training the LightGBM model. Each model is then pickle dumped (saved). We also extract feature importance from each model in order to consolidate it into a file and then aggregate it, resulting in having the mean importance across all the stores for that prediction horizon for each feature.

Exercise 5

Analyze the different feature importance reports from each model. Can you plot them and look for any common patterns? What can you understand of the model behavior as it has to deal with predictions further and further in time?

Exercise Notes (write down any notes or workings that will help you):

Here is the complete function for training all the models for a specific prediction horizon:

```python
def train(train_df, seed, end_train_day_x, predict_horizon):

    lgb_params = {
            'boosting_type': 'goss',
            'objective': 'tweedie',
            'tweedie_variance_power': 1.1,
            'metric': 'rmse',
            #'subsample': 0.5,
            #'subsample_freq': 1,
            'learning_rate': 0.03,
            'num_leaves': 2 ** 11 - 1,
            'min_data_in_leaf': 2 ** 12 - 1,
            'feature_fraction': 0.5,
            'max_bin': 100,
            'boost_from_average': False,
            'num_boost_round': 1400,
            'verbose': -1,
            'num_threads': os.cpu_count(),
            'force_row_wise': True,
        }

    random.seed(seed)
    np.random.seed(seed)
    os.environ['PYTHONHASHSEED'] = str(seed)

    lgb_params['seed'] = seed

    store_id_set_list = list(train_df['store_id'].unique())
    print(f"training stores: {store_id_set_list}")

    feature_importance_all_df = pd.DataFrame()
    for store_index, store_id in enumerate(store_id_set_list):
        print(f'now training {store_id} store')

        grid_df, enable_features = load_grid_by_store(end_train_day_x,
predict_horizon, store_id)
```

```
        train_mask = grid_df['d'] <= end_train_day_x
        valid_mask = train_mask & (grid_df['d'] > (end_train_day_x -
predict_horizon))
        preds_mask = grid_df['d'] > (end_train_day_x - 100)

        train_data = lgb.Dataset(grid_df[train_mask][enable_features],
                                 label=grid_df[train_mask]['sales'])

        valid_data = lgb.Dataset(grid_df[valid_mask][enable_features],
                                 label=grid_df[valid_mask]['sales'])


        # Saving part of the dataset for later predictions
        # Removing features that we need to calculate recursively
        grid_df = grid_df[preds_mask].reset_index(drop=True)
        grid_df.to_feather(f'test_{store_id}_{predict_horizon}.feather')
        del(grid_df)
        gc.collect()

        estimator = lgb.train(lgb_params,
                              train_data,
                              valid_sets=[valid_data],
                              callbacks=[lgb.log_evaluation(period=100,
show_stdv=False)],
                              )

        model_name = str(f'lgb_model_{store_id}_{predict_horizon}.bin')
        feature_importance_store_df = pd.DataFrame(sorted(zip(enable_
features, estimator.feature_importance())),
                                                   columns=['feature_
name', 'importance'])
        feature_importance_store_df = feature_importance_store_df.sort_
values('importance', ascending=False)
        feature_importance_store_df['store_id'] = store_id
        feature_importance_store_df.to_csv(f'feature_importance_{store_
id}_{predict_horizon}.csv', index=False)
```

```
        feature_importance_all_df = pd.concat([feature_importance_all_df,
    feature_importance_store_df])
        pickle.dump(estimator, open(model_name, 'wb'))

        del([train_data, valid_data, estimator])
        gc.collect()

    feature_importance_all_df.to_csv(f'feature_importance_all_{predict_
horizon}.csv', index=False)
    feature_importance_agg_df = feature_importance_all_df.groupby(
        'feature_name')['importance'].agg(['mean', 'std']).reset_index()
    feature_importance_agg_df.columns = ['feature_name', 'importance_
mean', 'importance_std']
    feature_importance_agg_df = feature_importance_agg_df.sort_
values('importance_mean', ascending=False)
    feature_importance_agg_df.to_csv(f'feature_importance_agg_{predict_
horizon}.csv', index=False)
```

With the last function prepared, we got all the necessary code up for our pipeline to work. For the function wrapping the whole operations together, we need the input datasets (the time series dataset, the price dataset, and the calendar information) together with the last training day (1,913 for predicting on the public leaderboard, and 1,941 for the private one) and the prediction horizon (which could be 7, 14, 21 or 28 days):

```
def train_pipeline(train_df, prices_df, calendar_df,
                    end_train_day_x_list, prediction_horizon_list):

    for end_train_day_x in end_train_day_x_list:

        for predict_horizon in prediction_horizon_list:

            print(f"end training point day: {end_train_day_x} - prediction
horizon: {predict_horizon} days")

            # Data preparation
            generate_base_grid(train_df, end_train_day_x, predict_horizon)
            calc_release_week(prices_df, end_train_day_x, predict_horizon)
            generate_grid_price(prices_df, calendar_df, end_train_day_x,
predict_horizon)
```

```
        generate_grid_calendar(calendar_df, end_train_day_x, predict_
    horizon)

        modify_grid_base(end_train_day_x, predict_horizon)

        generate_lag_feature(end_train_day_x, predict_horizon)

        generate_target_encoding_feature(end_train_day_x, predict_
    horizon)

        assemble_grid_by_store(train_df, end_train_day_x, predict_
    horizon)


    # Modelling
    train(train_df, seed, end_train_day_x, predict_horizon)
```

Since Kaggle notebooks have a limited running time and a limited amount of both memory and disk space, our suggested strategy is to replicate four notebooks with the code hereby presented and train them with different prediction horizon parameters. Using the same name for the notebooks but for a part containing the value of the prediction parameter will help in gathering and handling the models later as external datasets in another notebook. Each of these notebooks will take about 6 and a half hours to complete its run on a standard Kaggle notebook.

Here is the first notebook, *m5-train-day-1941-horizon-7* (`https://www.kaggle.com/code/lucamassaron/m5-train-day-1941-horizon-7`):

```
end_train_day_x_list = [1941]
prediction_horizon_list = [7]
seed = 42


train_pipeline(train_df, prices_df, calendar_df, end_train_day_x_list,
prediction_horizon_list)
```

The second notebook, *m5-train-day-1941-horizon-14* (`https://www.kaggle.com/code/lucamassaron/m5-train-day-1941-horizon-14`):

```
end_train_day_x_list = [1941]
prediction_horizon_list = [14]
seed = 42


train_pipeline(train_df, prices_df, calendar_df, end_train_day_x_list,
prediction_horizon_list)
```

The third notebook, *m5-train-day-1941-horizon-21* (`https://www.kaggle.com/code/lucamassaron/m5-train-day-1941-horizon-21`):

```
end_train_day_x_list = [1941]
prediction_horizon_list = [21]
seed = 42


train_pipeline(train_df, prices_df, calendar_df, end_train_day_x_list,
prediction_horizon_list)
```

Finally the last one, *m5-train-day-1941-horizon-28* (`https://www.kaggle.com/code/lucamassaron/m5-train-day-1941-horizon-28`):

```
end_train_day_x_list = [1941]
prediction_horizon_list = [28]
seed = 42


train_pipeline(train_df, prices_df, calendar_df, end_train_day_x_list,
prediction_horizon_list)
```

If you are working on a local computer with enough disk space and memory resources, you can just run all four prediction horizons together, by using the list containing them all, [7, 14, 21, 28], as input. Now, the last step before being able to submit our prediction is assembling the predictions.

Assembling public and private predictions

You can see an example of how we assembled the predictions for both the public and private leaderboards here:

- Public leaderboard example: `https://www.kaggle.com/lucamassaron/m5-predict-public-leaderboard`
- Private leaderboard example: `https://www.kaggle.com/code/lucamassaron/m5-predict-private-leaderboard`

What changes between the public and private submissions is just the different last training day: it determines what days we are going to predict. The public leaderboard notebook has the last training day set to 1,913, and the private one has it set to 1,941. You can actually, just for validation purposes, create other versions of the public version notebook using these dates for creating past holdout validation sets: [1885, 1857, 1829, 1577]. Hence the notebook will produce predictions that you can test locally for confirming the predictive capability of the model.

Exercise 6

Please try different holdout periods and record the validation scores. How does the model behave? Is it confirmed that it also works fine (it is a robust solution) in the past?

Exercise Notes (write down any notes or workings that will help you):

In this conclusive code snippet, after loading the necessary packages, such as LightGBM, for every end of a training day, and for every prediction horizon, we recover the correct notebook with its data. Then, we iterate through all the stores and predict the sales for all the items in the time ranging from the previous prediction horizon up to the present one. In this way, every model will predict on a single week, the one it has been trained on:

```python
import numpy as np
import pandas as pd
import os
import random
import math
from decimal import Decimal as dec
import datetime
import time
import gc
import lightgbm as lgb
import pickle

import warnings
warnings.filterwarnings("ignore", category=UserWarning)

store_id_set_list = ['CA_1', 'CA_2', 'CA_3', 'CA_4', 'TX_1', 'TX_2',
'TX_3', 'WI_1', 'WI_2', 'WI_3']
end_train_day_x_list = [1913, 1941]
prediction_horizon_list = [7, 14, 21, 28]

pred_v_all_df = list()

for end_train_day_x in end_train_day_x_list:
    previous_prediction_horizon = 0
    for prediction_horizon in prediction_horizon_list:
        notebook_name = f"../input/m5-train-day-{end_train_day_x}-horizon-
{prediction_horizon}"

        pred_v_df = pd.DataFrame()

        for store_index, store_id in enumerate(store_id_set_list):
```

```
        model_path = str(f'{notebook_name}/lgb_model_{store_id}_
{prediction_horizon}.bin')
        print(f'loading {model_path}')
        estimator = pickle.load(open(model_path, 'rb'))
        base_test = pd.read_feather(f"{notebook_name}/test_{store_id}_
{prediction_horizon}.feather")
        enable_features = [col for col in base_test.columns if col not
in ['id', 'd', 'sales']]


        for predict_day in range(previous_prediction_horizon + 1,
prediction_horizon + 1):
            print('[{3} -> {4}] predict {0}/{1} {2} day {5}'.format(
            store_index + 1, len(store_id_set_list), store_id,
            previous_prediction_horizon + 1, prediction_horizon,
predict_day))
            mask = base_test['d'] == (end_train_day_x + predict_day)
            base_test.loc[mask, 'sales'] = estimator.predict(base_
test[mask][enable_features])


        temp_v_df = base_test[
            (base_test['d'] >= end_train_day_x + previous_
prediction_horizon + 1) &
            (base_test['d'] < end_train_day_x + prediction_horizon
+ 1)
            ][['id', 'd', 'sales']]


        if len(pred_v_df)!=0:
            pred_v_df = pd.concat([pred_v_df, temp_v_df])
        else:
            pred_v_df = temp_v_df.copy()


        del(temp_v_df)
        gc.collect()


    previous_prediction_horizon = prediction_horizon
    pred_v_all_df.append(pred_v_df)


pred_v_all_df = pd.concat(pred_v_all_df)
```

When all the predictions have been gathered, we merge them using the sample submission file as a reference, both for the required rows to be predicted and for the columns format (Kaggle expects distinct rows for items in the validation or testing periods with daily sales in progressive columns):

```
submission = pd.read_csv("../input/m5-forecasting-accuracy/sample_
submission.csv")
pred_v_all_df.d = pred_v_all_df.d - end_train_day_x_list
pred_h_all_df = pred_v_all_df.pivot(index='id', columns='d',
values='sales')
pred_h_all_df = pred_h_all_df.reset_index()
pred_h_all_df.columns = submission.columns
submission = submission[['id']].merge(pred_h_all_df, on=['id'],
how='left').fillna(0)
submission.to_csv("m5_predictions.csv", index=False)
```

The solution can reach around 0.54907 in the private leaderboard, resulting in a 12th position, a placement in the final ranking inside the gold medal area. Reverting back to Monsaraida's LightGBM parameters (for instance, using gbdt instead of goss for the boosting parameter) should result in even higher performances (but you would need to run the code on a local computer or on Google Cloud Platform).

Exercise 7

If you have a local machine or cloud computing available and you can wait for training that may well exceed 12 hours, as an exercise, try comparing the training of LightGBM using the same number of iterations with the boosting set to gbdt instead of goss. How much is the difference in performance and training time?

Exercise Notes (write down any notes or workings that will help you):

Summary

In this second chapter, we took on quite a complex time series competition, hence the easiest top solution we tried is actually fairly complex, and it requires coding quite a lot of processing functions. After going through the chapter, you should have a better idea of how to process time series and have them predicted using gradient boosting. Favoring gradient-boosting solutions over traditional methods when you have enough data, as with this problem, should help you create strong solutions for complex problems with hierarchical correlations, intermittent series, and availability of covariates such as events, prices, or market conditions.

In the following chapters, you will tackle even more complex Kaggle competitions, dealing with images and text. You will be amazed at how much you can learn by recreating top-scoring solutions and understanding their inner workings.

Join our book's Discord space

Join our Discord community to meet like-minded people and learn alongside more than 2000 members at:

```
https://packt.link/KaggleDiscord
```

3

Vision Competition — Cassava Leaf Disease Competition

In this chapter, we will leave the domain of tabular data and focus on computer vision. In order to demonstrate the steps necessary to do well in classification competitions, we will use the data from the Cassava Leaf Disease contest: `https://www.kaggle.com/competitions/cassava-leaf-disease-classification`.

The first thing to do upon starting a Kaggle competition is to read the description properly:

> "As the second-largest provider of carbohydrates in Africa, cassava is a key food security crop grown by smallholder farmers because it can withstand harsh conditions. At least 80% of household farms in Sub-Saharan Africa grow this starchy root, but viral diseases are major sources of poor yields. With the help of data science, it may be possible to identify common diseases so they can be treated."

So this competition relates to an important real-life problem:

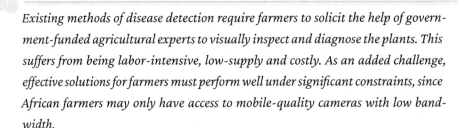

> *Existing methods of disease detection require farmers to solicit the help of government-funded agricultural experts to visually inspect and diagnose the plants. This suffers from being labor-intensive, low-supply and costly. As an added challenge, effective solutions for farmers must perform well under significant constraints, since African farmers may only have access to mobile-quality cameras with low bandwidth.*

This paragraph – especially the last sentence – sets the expectations: since the data is coming from diverse sources, we are likely to have some challenges related to quality of the images and (possibly) distribution shift.

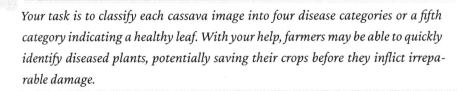

> *Your task is to classify each cassava image into four disease categories or a fifth category indicating a healthy leaf. With your help, farmers may be able to quickly identify diseased plants, potentially saving their crops before they inflict irreparable damage.*

This bit is rather important: it specifies that this is a classification competition, and the number of classes is small (5 in this case).

In this chapter, you will learn:

- The competition data and metrics
- How to build a baseline model
- Insights from the top solutions

With the introductory footwork out of the way, let us have a look at the data.

  The code files for this chapter can be found at `https://packt.link/kwbchp3`.

Understanding the data and metrics

Upon entering the **Data** tab for this competition, we see the summary of the provided data:

Dataset Description

Can you identify a problem with a cassava plant using a photo from a relatively inexpensive camera? This competition will challenge you to distinguish between several diseases that cause material harm to the food supply of many African countries. In some cases the main remedy is to burn the infected plants to prevent further spread, which can make a rapid automated turnaround quite useful to the farmers.

Files

[train/test]_images the image files. The full set of test images will only be available to your notebook when it is submitted for scoring. Expect to see roughly 15,000 images in the test set.

train.csv

- `image_id` the image file name.
- `label` the ID code for the disease.

sample_submission.csv A properly formatted sample submission, given the disclosed test set content.

- `image_id` the image file name.
- `label` the predicted ID code for the disease.

[train/test]_tfrecords the image files in tfrecord format.

label_num_to_disease_map.json The mapping between each disease code and the real disease name.

Figure 3.1: Description of the Cassava competition dataset

What can we make of that?

- The data is in a fairly straightforward format, where the organizers even provided the mapping between disease names and numerical codes .

- We have the data in TFRecord format, which is good news for anyone interested in using a TPU.

- The provided test set is only a small subset of the actual test set used for evaluation, and the former is substituted with the latter at submission evaluation time. **This suggests that loading a previously trained model at evaluation time and using it for inference is the preferred strategy.**

Categorization accuracy (`https://developers.google.com/machine-learning/crash-course/classification/accuracy`) was chosen as the evaluation metric:

accuracy = (number of correct predictions)/(total number of predictions)

This metric takes discrete values as inputs, which means potential ensemble strategies become somewhat more involved. Ensembling is the process of combining the predictions of multiple models to create a more accurate prediction. When ensembling metrics with discrete values, such as classification labels, it can be harder than ensembling metrics with continuous values, such as real-valued numbers. This is because the output of the models being combined must be the same type in order to be combined, and combining discrete values is more difficult than combining continuous values.

For example, when ensembling classification models, the outputs of the individual models must be combined in a way that preserves the discrete nature of the classification labels. This can be challenging because it is not always clear how to combine the outputs of multiple models in a way that is both accurate and maintains the discrete nature of the classification labels. In contrast, when ensembling regression models, the outputs of the individual models can be combined by simply taking the average of the predictions, which is a straightforward operation that preserves the continuous nature of the output.

The loss function is implemented during training to optimize the learning function and as long as we want to use methods based on gradient descent, this one needs to be continuous. The evaluation metric, on the other hand, is used after training to measure overall performance and as such, can be discrete.

Exercise 1

Without building a model, write a code to conduct a basic EDA.

Compare the cardinality of classes in our classification problem.

Exercise Notes (write down any notes or workings that will help you):

Normally, this would also be the moment to check for distribution shift: the difference in the underlying distribution of the training and test data for a machine learning model. In the context of image classification, this can manifest in a number of ways: the training data may contain images of a particular type or from a specific location, while the test data contains images that are different in some way. This can lead to a situation where the model performs well on the training data but poorly on the test data, because the model has not seen examples of the types of images that are present in the test set.

To address this issue, it is important to ensure that the training and test data are representative of the real-world distribution of data that the model will encounter when it is deployed. There are three main approaches to mitigating the impact of concept drift in practice:

- Regularization helps mitigate the impact of distributional changes in the data
- Augmentations designed to mimic the changes in the distribution: as an example, if we suspect test data might contain images taken with lower-quality cameras, we can introduce noise to the original photos
- Adversarial validation: please check *Chapter 6* of *The Kaggle Book* for a discussion of adversarial validation, which is a popular technique for detecting concept drift between datasets

However, since we do not have access to the complete dataset in this case, this step is omitted and mentioned primarily for completeness of exposition.

Building a baseline model

We start our approach by building a baseline solution. The notebook running an end-to-end solution is available at: `https://www.kaggle.com/code/konradb/ch3-end-to-end-image-classification`.

While hopefully useful as a starting point for other competitions you might want to try, it is more educational to follow the flow described in this section, i.e., copying the code cell by cell, so that you can understand it better (and of course improve on it – it is called a baseline solution for a reason):

```
import numpy as np
import pandas as pd
import matplotlib.pyplot as plt
import seaborn as sns
import datetime

from sklearn.model_selection import train_test_split
```

```
from sklearn.metrics import accuracy_score
import tensorflow as tf
from tensorflow.keras import models, layers
from tensorflow.keras.preprocessing import image
from tensorflow.keras.preprocessing.image import ImageDataGenerator
from tensorflow.keras.callbacks import ModelCheckpoint, EarlyStopping,
ReduceLROnPlateau
from tensorflow.keras.applications import EfficientNetB0
from tensorflow.keras.optimizers import Adam

# ignoring warnings
import warnings
warnings.simplefilter("ignore")

import os, cv2, json
from PIL import Image
```

We begin by importing the necessary packages – while personal differences in style are a natural thing, it is our opinion that gathering the imports in one place makes the code easier to maintain as the competition progresses and you move toward more elaborate solutions. In addition, we create a configuration class – a placeholder for all the parameters characterizing our learning process:

```
class CFG:
    # config
    WORK_DIR = '../input/cassava-leaf-disease-classification'
    BATCH_SIZE = 8
    EPOCHS = 5
    TARGET_SIZE = 256
    NCLASSES = 5
```

The components include:

- The data folder is mostly useful if you train models outside of Kaggle sometimes (for example, in Google Colab or on your local machine)

- BATCH_SIZE is a parameter that sometimes needs adjusting if you want to optimize your training process (or make it possible at all, for large images in constrained memory environment)

- Modifying EPOCHS is useful for debugging: start with a small number of epochs to verify that your solution is running smoothly from end to end and increase as you are moving towards a proper solution
- TARGET_SIZE defines the size to which you want to rescale your images
- NCLASSES corresponds to the number of possible classes in your classification problem

A good practice for coding a solution is to encapsulate the important bits in functions – and creating our trainable model certainly qualifies as important:

```
def create_model():
    conv_base = EfficientNetB0(include_top = False, weights = None,
                               input_shape = (CFG.TARGET_SIZE, CFG.TARGET_
SIZE, 3))
    model = conv_base.output
    model = layers.GlobalAveragePooling2D()(model)
    model = layers.Dense(CFG.NCLASSES, activation = "softmax")(model)
    model = models.Model(conv_base.input, model)

    model.compile(optimizer = Adam(lr = 0.001),
                  loss = "sparse_categorical_crossentropy",
                  metrics = ["acc"])
    return model
```

A few remarks about this step:

- While more expressive options are available, it is practical to begin with a fast model that can be quickly iterated upon. The EfficientNet (https://paperswithcode.com/method/efficientnet) architecture fits the bill quite well.
- We add a pooling layer for regularization purposes.
- Add a classification head – a Dense layer with CFG.NCLASSES indicating the number of possible results for the classifier.
- Finally, we compile the model with the loss and metrics corresponding to the requirements for this competition.

Exercise 2

Examine the possible choices for the loss and metric – a useful guide is `https://keras.io/api/losses/`.

What would the other reasonable options be?

Exercise Notes (write down any notes or workings that will help you):

The next step is the data:

```
train_labels = pd.read_csv(os.path.join(CFG.WORK_DIR, "train.csv"))

STEPS_PER_EPOCH = len(train_labels)*0.8 / CFG.BATCH_SIZE
VALIDATION_STEPS = len(train_labels)*0.2 / CFG.BATCH_SIZE

train_labels.label = train_labels.label.astype('str')
train_datagen = ImageDataGenerator(validation_split = 0.2, preprocessing_
function = None,
                                   rotation_range = 45, zoom_range =
0.2,
                                   horizontal_flip = True, vertical_flip
= True,
                                   fill_mode = 'nearest', shear_range =
0.1,
                                   height_shift_range = 0.1, width_
shift_range = 0.1)

train_generator = train_datagen.flow_from_dataframe(train_labels,
directory = os.path.join(CFG.WORK_DIR, "train_images"),
                        subset = "training", x_col = "image_id",
                        y_col = "label", target_size = (CFG.TARGET_SIZE,
CFG.TARGET_SIZE),
                        batch_size = CFG.BATCH_SIZE, class_mode =
"sparse")


validation_datagen = ImageDataGenerator(validation_split = 0.2)

validation_generator = validation_datagen.flow_from_dataframe(train_
labels,
                        directory = os.path.join(CFG.WORK_DIR, "train_
images"),
                        subset = "validation", x_col = "image_id",
                        y_col = "label", target_size = (CFG.TARGET_SIZE,
CFG.TARGET_SIZE),
                        batch_size = CFG.BATCH_SIZE, class_mode =
"sparse")
```

Next, we set up the model – this is straightforward, thanks to the function we defined above:

```
model = create_model()
model.summary()
```

Before we proceed to training the model, we should dedicate some attention to callbacks:

```
model_save = ModelCheckpoint('./EffNetB0_512_8_best_weights.h5',
                             save_best_only = True,
                             save_weights_only = True,
                             monitor = 'val_loss',
                             mode = 'min', verbose = 1)
early_stop = EarlyStopping(monitor = 'val_loss', min_delta = 0.001,
                           patience = 5, mode = 'min', verbose = 1,
                           restore_best_weights = True)
reduce_lr = ReduceLROnPlateau(monitor = 'val_loss', factor = 0.3,
                              patience = 2, min_delta = 0.001,
                              mode = 'min', verbose = 1)
```

Some points worth mentioning:

- ModelCheckpoint is used to ensure we keep the weights for the best model only, where the optimality is determined by the metric to monitor (validation loss in this instance).

- The EarlyStopping callback in Keras is a method for automatically stopping the training of a deep learning model when the model's performance on a validation set stops improving. This can be useful because it allows the training process to be terminated before the model overfits to the training data, which can lead to poor performance on new, unseen data. The EarlyStopping callback is typically used in conjunction with other techniques, such as regularization and learning rate schedules, to improve the performance of a deep learning model.

- The ReduceLROnPlateau schema is a learning rate schedule in Keras that reduces the learning rate of a model when the model's performance on a validation set plateaus. This means that the model's performance stops improving over a certain number of epochs. When this happens, the ReduceLROnPlateau schema will reduce the learning rate by a specified factor, allowing the model to continue learning but at a slower pace. This can help prevent the model from overfitting and can also help the model to converge on a solution more quickly.

Exercise 3

What parameters would it make sense to modify in the above setup, and which ones can be left at their default values?

Exercise Notes (write down any notes or workings that will help you):

An excellent starting point for hyperparameter tuning with TensorFlow can be found in the official documentation:

```
https://www.tensorflow.org/tutorials/keras/keras_tuner
```

With this set up, we can fit the model:

```
history = model.fit(
    train_generator,
    steps_per_epoch = STEPS_PER_EPOCH,
    epochs = CFG.EPOCHS,
    validation_data = validation_generator,
    validation_steps = VALIDATION_STEPS,
    callbacks = [model_save, early_stop, reduce_lr]
)
```

Once the training is complete, we can use the model to build a prediction of the image class for each image in the test set. Recall that, in this competition, the public (visible) test set consisted of a single image and the size of the full one was unknown – hence the need for a slightly convoluted manner of constructing the submission DataFrame:

```
submit_df = pd.read_csv(os.path.join(CFG.WORK_DIR, "sample_submission.
csv"))

preds = []

for image_id in submit_df.image_id:
    image = Image.open(os.path.join(CFG.WORK_DIR,  "test_images", image_
id))
    image = image.resize((CFG.TARGET_SIZE, CFG.TARGET_SIZE))
    image = np.expand_dims(image, axis = 0)
    preds.append(np.argmax(model.predict(image)))

submit_df ['label'] = preds
submit_df.to_csv('submission.csv', index = False)
```

In this section, we have demonstrated how to start competing in a competition focused on image classification – you can use this approach to move quickly from basic EDA to a functional submission. However, a rudimentary approach like this is unlikely to produce very competitive results.

For this reason, in the next section, we discuss more specialized techniques that were utilized in top-scoring solutions.

Learning from top solutions

In this section, we gather aspects of the top solutions that could allow us to rise above the level of the baseline solution. Keep in mind that the leaderboards (both public and private) in this competition were quite tight; this was due to a combination of a couple of factors:

- Noisy data: it was easy to get to 0.89 accuracy by correctly identifying a large part of the train data, and then each new correct one allowed for a tiny move upward
- Limited size of the data

Pretraining

The first and most obvious remedy to the issue of limited data size was pretraining: using more data. Pretraining a deep learning model on more data can be beneficial because it can help the model learn better representations of the data, which can in turn improve the performance of the model on downstream tasks. When a deep learning model is trained on a large dataset, it can learn to extract useful features from the data that are relevant to the task at hand. This can provide a strong foundation for the model, allowing it to learn more effectively when it is fine-tuned on a smaller, specific dataset.

Additionally, pretraining on a large dataset can help the model to generalize better to new, unseen data. Because the model has seen a wide range of examples during pretraining, it can better adapt to new data that may be different from the training data in some way. This can be especially important when working with deep learning models, which can have a large number of parameters and can be difficult to train effectively from scratch.

The Cassava competition was held a year before as well: `https://www.kaggle.com/competitions/ cassava-disease/overview`.

With minimal adjustments, the data from the 2019 edition could be leveraged in the context of the current one. Several competitors addressed the topic:

- A combined 2019 + 2020 dataset in TFRecords format was released in the Kaggle forum: `https://www.kaggle.com/competitions/cassava-leaf-disease-classification/ discussion/199131`
- The winning solution from the 2019 edition served as a useful starting point: `https://www.kaggle.com/competitions/cassava-leaf-disease-classification/ discussion/216985`

- Generating predictions on 2019 data and using the pseudo-labels to augment the dataset was reported to yield some (minor) improvements: `https://www.kaggle.com/competitions/cassava-leaf-disease-classification/discussion/203594`

Test time augmentation

The idea behind **Test Time Augmentation (TTA)** is to apply different transformations to the test image: rotations, flipping, and translations. This creates a few different versions of the test image, and we generate a prediction for each of them. The resulting class probabilities are then averaged to get a more confident answer. An excellent demonstration of this technique is given in a notebook by Andrew Khael: `https://www.kaggle.com/code/andrewkh/test-time-augmentation-tta-worth-it`.

TTA was used extensively by the top solutions in the Cassava competition, an excellent example being the top three private leaderboard results: `https://www.kaggle.com/competitions/cassava-leaf-disease-classification/discussion/221150`.

Transformers

While more widely known architectures like ResNeXt and EfficientNet were used a lot in the course of the competition, it was the addition of more novel ones that provided the extra edge to many competitors yearning for progress in a tightly packed leaderboard. Transformers emerged in 2017 as a revolutionary architecture for NLP (if somehow you missed the paper that started it all, here it is: `https://arxiv.org/abs/1706.03762`) and were such a spectacular success that, inevitably, many people started wondering if they could be applied to other modalities as well – vision being an obvious candidate. The aptly named **Vision Transformer (ViT)** made one of its first appearances in a Kaggle competition in the Cassava contest.

An excellent tutorial for ViT has been made public: `https://www.kaggle.com/code/abhinand05/vision-transformer-vit-tutorial-baseline`.

Ensembling

Ensembling is very popular on Kaggle (see *Chapter 9* of *The Kaggle Book* for a more elaborate description) and the Cassava competition was no exception. As it turned out, combining diverse architectures was very beneficial (by averaging the class probabilities): EfficientNet, ResNext, and ViT are sufficiently different from each other that their predictions complement each other. When building a machine learning ensemble, it is useful to combine models that are different from one another because this can help improve the overall performance of the ensemble.

Ensembling is the process of combining the predictions of multiple models to create a more accurate prediction. By combining models that have different strengths and weaknesses, the ensemble can take advantage of the strengths of each individual model to make more accurate predictions.

For example, if the individual models in an ensemble are all based on the same type of algorithm, they may all make similar errors on certain types of data. By combining models that use different algorithms, the ensemble can potentially correct for the errors made by each individual model, leading to better overall performance. Additionally, by combining models that have been trained on different data or using different parameters, the ensemble can potentially capture more of the underlying variation in the data, leading to more accurate predictions.

Another important approach was stacking, i.e., using models in two stages. First we construct multiple predictions from diverse models, and those are subsequently used as input for a second-level model: `https://www.kaggle.com/competitions/cassava-leaf-disease-classification/discussion/220751`.

The winning solution involved a different approach (with fewer models in the final blend), but relied on the same core logic: `https://www.kaggle.com/competitions/cassava-leaf-disease-classification/discussion/221957`.

A complete solution

Earlier in this chapter, we described how to get started with a baseline solution for an image classification competition. In this section, we show how an ensemble team involving rockstars, such as Abhishek (`https://www.kaggle.com/abhishek`) and Tanul (`https://www.kaggle.com/tanulsingh077`), achieved a silver medal zone solution (36th) using a cleverly structured application of the components discussed above. The post summarizing their solution can be found here: `https://www.kaggle.com/competitions/cassava-leaf-disease-classification/discussion/220628`.

Their final solution was a combination of three models: `EfficientNet-B7`, `EfficientNet-B3a`, and `SE-ResNext50`. The models followed the pipeline described in the notebook: `https://www.kaggle.com/code/abhishek/tez-faster-and-easier-training-for-leaf-detection/`. A notable thing about this notebook is that it utilizes tez: a PyTorch trainer developed by Abhishek (`https://github.com/abhishekkrthakur/tez`). The idea behind tez is to simplify the creation and deployment of PyTorch models by removing the need for boilerplate code. This objective is achieved by standardizing the core components of the pipeline: first, the model class.

Below, we discuss some parts of the solution demonstrated in https://www.kaggle.com/code/ abhishek/tez-faster-and-easier-training-for-leaf-detection/:

```python
class LeafModel(tez.Model):
    def __init__(self, num_classes):
        super().__init__()

        self.effnet = EfficientNet.from_pretrained("efficientnet-b4")
        self.dropout = nn.Dropout(0.1)
        self.out = nn.Linear(1792, num_classes)
        self.step_scheduler_after = "epoch"

    def monitor_metrics(self, outputs, targets):
        if targets is None:
            return {}
        outputs = torch.argmax(outputs, dim=1).cpu().detach().numpy()
        targets = targets.cpu().detach().numpy()
        accuracy = metrics.accuracy_score(targets, outputs)
        return {"accuracy": accuracy}

    def fetch_optimizer(self):
        opt = torch.optim.Adam(self.parameters(), lr=3e-4)
        return opt

    def fetch_scheduler(self):
        sch = torch.optim.lr_scheduler.CosineAnnealingWarmRestarts(
            self.optimizer, T_0=10, T_mult=1, eta_min=1e-6, last_epoch=-1
        )
        return sch

    def forward(self, image, targets=None):
        batch_size, _, _, _ = image.shape

        x = self.effnet.extract_features(image)
        x = F.adaptive_avg_pool2d(x, 1).reshape(batch_size, -1)
        outputs = self.out(self.dropout(x))
```

```
       if targets is not None:
           loss = nn.CrossEntropyLoss()(outputs, targets)
           metrics = self.monitor_metrics(outputs, targets)
           return outputs, loss, metrics
       return outputs, None, None
```

What does this code do? Let's go through the components:

1. The first block defines the model architecture in PyTorch fashion: pretrained body, followed by dropout regularization, and a classification head geared to our task.

2. This is followed by the monitor_metrics method, which, in our case, returns the model accuracy.

3. The two methods after that are optional (default optimizer values are frequently acceptable; the most important parameter to tune is the learning rate).

4. Finally, we have the forward method, which defines how our model is going to be run from input to output.

The advantage of a framework like tez is that it enforces repeatable structure in the models, allowing us to do away with boilerplate code.

Another useful feature of tez, demonstrated in this solution, is the ImageDataset functionality – it simplifies the process of data structure creation, which can be at times overwhelming for newcomers used to the scikit-learn way of doing things:

```
image_path = "../input/cassava-leaf-disease-classification/train_images/"
train_image_paths = [os.path.join(image_path, x) for x in df_train.image_
id.values]
valid_image_paths = [os.path.join(image_path, x) for x in df_valid.image_
id.values]
train_targets = df_train.label.values
valid_targets = df_valid.label.values

train_dataset = ImageDataset(
    image_paths=train_image_paths,
    targets=train_targets,
    resize=None,
    augmentations=train_aug,
)
```

```
valid_dataset = ImageDataset(
    image_paths=valid_image_paths,
    targets=valid_targets,
    resize=None,
    augmentations=valid_aug,
)
```

After splitting the dataset according to folds, we simply create two instances of the `ImageDataset` class, and the data processing is taken care of under the hood, with minimal need for user involvement. This allows us to concentrate on the actual modeling task instead of PyTorch debugging.

The model training is very straightforward and flexible – in particular, incorporating callbacks like early stopping will look familiar to anybody who has tried the Keras/TensorFlow approach to modeling before:

```
model = LeafModel(num_classes=dfx.label.nunique())

es = EarlyStopping(
    monitor="valid_loss", model_path="model.bin", patience=3, mode="min"
)

model.fit(
    train_dataset,
    valid_dataset=valid_dataset,
    train_bs=32,
    valid_bs=64,
    device="cuda",
    epochs=10,
    callbacks=[es],
    fp16=True,
)
model.save("model.bin")
```

In this section, we demonstrated parts of a silver medal zone solution that performed remarkably well by taking the elementary ideas introduced in our baseline, utilizing a PyTorch trainer, and ensembling different architectures trained on higher-resolution images.

Exercise 4

Suppose you have trained three different models (architectures). Can you think of cases when a majority vote may give an inferior performance to combining class probability vectors? What are the different ways of combining vectors of probabilities denoting class affiliation? Hint: start by comparing when a majority vote might lead to a different performance than pointwise mean, median, or other location measures.

Exercise Notes (write down any notes or workings that will help you):

Summary

In this chapter, we described how to get started with a baseline solution for an image classification competition and discussed a diverse set of possible extensions for moving to a competitive (medal) zone. In the next chapter, we will take a similar journey with NLP, demonstrating how to get started on a proper journey through a text classification competition.

Join our book's Discord space

Join our Discord community to meet like-minded people and learn alongside more than 2000 members at:

https://packt.link/KaggleDiscord

4

NLP Competition – Google Quest Q&A Labeling

In this chapter, we will talk about **Natural Language Processing (NLP)** applications – specifically, text classification. In order to demonstrate our approach, we will be using the data from the Google Quest Q&A Labeling contest: `https://www.kaggle.com/competitions/google-quest-challenge`.

What was this competition about? The following is the official description:

> Computers are really good at answering questions with single, verifiable answers. But humans are often still better at answering questions about opinions, recommendations, or personal experiences.

> Humans are better at addressing subjective questions that require a deeper, multi-dimensional understanding of context – something computers aren't trained to do well...yet. Questions can take many forms – some have multi-sentence elaborations, others may be simple curiosity or a fully developed problem. They can have multiple intents or seek advice and opinions. Some may be helpful and others interesting. Some are simple right or wrong.

> *Unfortunately, it's hard to build better subjective question-answering algorithms because of a lack of data and predictive models. That's why the CrowdSource team at Google Research, a group dedicated to advancing NLP and other types of ML science via crowdsourcing, has collected data on a number of these quality scoring aspects.*
>
> *In this competition, you're challenged to use this new dataset to build predictive algorithms for different subjective aspects of question-answering. The question-answer pairs were gathered from nearly 70 different websites, in a "common-sense" fashion. Our raters received minimal guidance and training, and relied largely on their subjective interpretation of the prompts. As such, each prompt was crafted in the most intuitive fashion so that raters could simply use their common sense to complete the task. By lessening our dependency on complicated and opaque rating guidelines, we hope to increase the re-use value of this dataset. What you see is what you get!*
>
> **Demonstrating these subjective labels can be predicted reliably can shine a new light on this research area.** *Results from this competition will inform the way future intelligent Q&A systems will get built, hopefully contributing to them becoming more human-like.*

What can we gather from this introduction? First, the algorithms we build here are supposed to mimic the feedback given by the human evaluator; since this feedback constitutes our ground truth, we can expect some noise in the labels. Second, there are multiple aspects of each answer to be predicted, and those are averaged across evaluators – which means our problem is likely to be well represented by multivariate regression.

We've structured this chapter similarly to the previous one about computer vision problems:

- We discuss how to start building a baseline solution
- We then examine the top-performing solutions

   The code for this chapter can be found at `https://packt.link/kwbchp4`.

The baseline solution

It is 2023, so just about everything in NLP starts with a transformer architecture – and when it comes to implementation, **Hugging Face (HF)** rules the field supreme. The Transformers library from HF is a popular open-source library for implementing state-of-the-art NLP models. It is built on top of the PyTorch library and provides a high-level interface for working with a variety of NLP tasks, such as language translation, text classification, and language generation.

One of the main features of the Transformers library is that it provides the ability to fine-tune large pretrained language models on specific tasks. These models, including multiple variants of BERT, as well as GPT, have been trained on massive datasets and are able to capture the patterns and structure of natural language with a high degree of accuracy. By fine-tuning these models on a specific task, users can leverage the pretrained knowledge of the model to achieve strong results with relatively little training data. The library also includes a wide range of tools for pre-processing and postprocessing text data, as well as utilities for training and evaluating models.

Our code starts by installing and importing the most recent version of the Transformers library:

```
!pip install transformers
import transformer
```

We follow up with the necessary imports:

```
import sys, glob, torch, random
import os, re, gc, pickle, string
import numpy as np
import pandas as pd
from scipy import stats

from transformers import DistilBertTokenizer,DistilBertModel
import math

from scipy.stats import spearmanr, rankdata
from os.path import join as path_join
from numpy.random import seed
from urllib.parse import urlparse
from sklearn.preprocessing import OneHotEncoder

seed(42)
random.seed(42)
```

This next group of imports gathers the different functionalities from scikit-learn. These will be used for feature extraction and normalization:

```
import nltk
from nltk.corpus import stopwords
from sklearn.base import clone
from sklearn.pipeline import Pipeline, FeatureUnion
from sklearn.preprocessing import StandardScaler, PowerTransformer,
RobustScaler, KBinsDiscretizer, QuantileTransformer
from sklearn.feature_extraction.text import TfidfVectorizer
from sklearn.compose import ColumnTransformer
from sklearn.model_selection import StratifiedKFold, GridSearchCV, KFold,
GroupKFold
from sklearn.multioutput import MultiOutputRegressor
from sklearn.impute import SimpleImputer
from sklearn.metrics import make_scorer
from sklearn.multiclass import OneVsRestClassifier
from sklearn.linear_model import LinearRegression, Ridge
from sklearn.svm import LinearSVR, SVR


eng_stopwords = set(stopwords.words("english"))


import tensorflow as tf
import tensorflow_hub as hub
```

We specify some general settings:

```
# settings
data_dir = '../input/google-quest-challenge/'
RANDOM_STATE = 42


import datetime
```

Our strategy in building a baseline solution is to construct a large space of features summarizing the data – so examining the dataset first is a good initial step. *Figure 4.1* shows a few top rows of the dataset as a sample:

question_title	question_body	question_user_name	question_user_page	answer
What am I losing when using extension tubes in...	After playing around with macro photography on...	ysap	https://photo.stackexchange.com/users/1024	I just got extension tubes, so here's the skin...
What is the distinction between a city and a s...	I am trying to understand what kinds of places...	russellpierce	https://rpg.stackexchange.com/users/8774	It might be helpful to look into the definitio...
Maximum protusion length for through-hole comp...	I'm working on a PCB that has through-hole com...	Joe Baker	https://electronics.stackexchange.com/users/10157	Do you even need grooves? We make several pro...
Can an affidavit be used in Beit Din?	An affidavit, from what i understand, is basic...	Scimonster	https://judaism.stackexchange.com/users/5151	Sending an "affidavit" it is a dispute between...

Figure 4.1: Sample rows from the training data

For each row, we have the question title, the question body, and the answer – followed by the target columns (which are reported below), summarizing the views expressed by the human evaluators. We specify our target columns of interest:

```
target_cols = ['question_asker_intent_understanding', 'question_body_
critical',
                'question_conversational', 'question_expect_short_answer',
                'question_fact_seeking', 'question_has_commonly_accepted_
answer',
                'question_interestingness_others', 'question_
interestingness_self',
                'question_multi_intent', 'question_not_really_a_question',
                'question_opinion_seeking', 'question_type_choice',
                'question_type_compare', 'question_type_consequence',
                'question_type_definition', 'question_type_entity',
                'question_type_instructions', 'question_type_procedure',
                'question_type_reason_explanation', 'question_type_
spelling',
```

```
                        'question_well_written', 'answer_helpful',
                        'answer_level_of_information', 'answer_plausible',
                        'answer_relevance', 'answer_satisfaction',
                        'answer_type_instructions', 'answer_type_procedure',
                        'answer_type_reason_explanation', 'answer_well_written']
```

For a complete explanation of the meaning and interpretation of those targets, check out the **Data** section of the competition: `https://www.kaggle.com/c/google-quest-challenge/data`

As mentioned earlier, we will focus on extracting the features from the question components, and to do that we need some helper functions. We begin with one of the simplest things you can do with a chunk of text, namely, count the words:

```
def word_count(xstring):
    return xstring.split().str.len()
```

Next, we turn our attention to the competition metric: Spearman's correlation is a measure of the statistical relationship between two variables. It is a nonparametric test that is used to determine the strength and direction of the relationship between two variables. Specifically, it measures the extent to which the two variables are correlated, and whether the relationship between them is positive (i.e., as one variable increases, the other variable also increases) or negative (i.e., as one variable increases, the other variable decreases). Spearman's correlation coefficient, denoted by the Greek letter *rho* (ρ), is calculated by taking the difference between the ranks of the two variables for each data point, squaring the differences, and summing them up. The coefficient can range from -1 to 1, with 0 indicating no relationship between the variables, 1 indicating a perfect positive correlation, and -1 indicating a perfect negative correlation. A Spearman's correlation coefficient close to 1 or -1 indicates a strong relationship between the variables, while a coefficient closer to 0 indicates a weaker relationship. The Spearman's correlation coefficient formula is as follows:

$$\rho\,(X,Y)\;=\;\frac{cov(R(X)\,,R(Y))}{\sigma(R(X))\sigma(R(Y))}$$

where:

- $R(X)$ and $R(Y)$ are the respective X and Y variables converted to ranks: `https://en.wikipedia.org/wiki/Ranking`
- *cov* is the covariance of the rank variables
- $\sigma(R(X))$ and $\sigma(R(Y))$ are the standard deviations of the rank variables

Spearman's correlation is often used when the data is not normally distributed or when the relationship between the variables is not linear – both of these are the case with our targets, which are normalized to the unit interval, and almost certainly related to the characteristics of the text in a non-linear fashion. It is also useful when working with ordinal data, or data that is ranked or ordered rather than measured on a continuous scale:

```
def spearman_corr(y_true, y_pred):
        if np.ndim(y_pred) == 2:
            corr = np.mean([stats.spearmanr(y_true[:, i], y_pred[:, i])[0]
for i in range(y_true.shape[1])])
        else:
            corr = stats.spearmanr(y_true, y_pred)[0]
        return corr


custom_scorer = make_scorer(spearman_corr, greater_is_better=True)
```

The last part, i.e., converting our function to a scorer, is necessary if we want to use Spearman's correlation inside a scikit-learn pipeline; `make_scorer` takes a scoring function and returns a callable that evaluates an output of the estimator.

Exercise 1

The competition metric was a new one for many participants in this competition; as such, it generated a lot of discussions and investigations into its difference from other metrics. Explore the discussions in the competition forum that focused on the Spearman correlation.

Exercise Notes (write down any notes or workings that will help you):

Next, we create a small helper function to extract successive chunks of size n from 1. This will help us later with generating embeddings for our body of text without running into memory problems:

```
def chunks(1, n):
for i in range(0, len(1), n):
        yield l[i:i + n]
```

Part of the feature set we will use is embeddings from pretrained models. Please recall that our aim here is to create a baseline – but the availability of large language models in recent years redefined the meaning of a baseline in NLP. Can we base our initial solution on a BERT-like model? We begin by defining a function to create embedding vectors, importing the tokenizer and model, and then we process the corpus in chunks, encoding each question/answer into a fixed-size embedding.

In an NLP model, the tokenizer is responsible for splitting the input text into individual tokens (words or sub-words) that can be fed into the model. The tokenizer first splits the input text into words using white space and punctuation as delimiters, and subsequently converts each word into its corresponding token using the BERT model vocabulary. This process is known as tokenization, and it is a crucial one in preparing text data for input into a BERT model. The tokenizer also adds special tokens at the end of each sentence, thus indicating the structure of the input text. The output of the tokenizer represents the sentence as a sequence of tokens that can be fed directly into the BERT model:

```
def fetch_vectors(string_list, batch_size=64):
    DEVICE = torch.device("cuda")
    tokenizer = transformers.DistilBertTokenizer.from_pretrained("../
input/distilbertbaseuncased/")
    model = transformers.DistilBertModel.from_pretrained("../input/
distilbertbaseuncased/")
    model.to(DEVICE)

    fin_features = []
    for data in chunks(string_list, batch_size):
        tokenized = []
        for x in data:
            x = " ".join(x.strip().split()[:300])
            tok = tokenizer.encode(x, add_special_tokens=True)
            tokenized.append(tok[:512])

        max_len = 512
```

```
        padded = np.array([i + [0] * (max_len - len(i)) for i in
tokenized])
        attention_mask = np.where(padded != 0, 1, 0)
        input_ids = torch.tensor(padded).to(DEVICE)
        attention_mask = torch.tensor(attention_mask).to(DEVICE)

        with torch.no_grad():
            last_hidden_states = model(input_ids, attention_
mask=attention_mask)

        features = last_hidden_states[0][:, 0, :].cpu().numpy()
        fin_features.append(features)

    fin_features = np.vstack(fin_features)
    return fin_features
```

Exercise 2

Inspect the differences between the different tokenizers used in the Transformers library: Byte-Pair, WordPiece, and SentencePiece. Could another choice have been better here? Hint: start with the Hugging Face documentation.

Exercise Notes (write down any notes or workings that will help you):

The function can be difficult to digest, so here is an explanation of the main steps in the flow:

1. Load the tokenizer and model from a checkpoint
2. Loop through the input strings in small batches (determined by the `batch_size` argument)
3. Split the input data into words, truncating the resulting collection at 300 elements
4. Tokenize the input data
5. Pad the tokenized input data, so that all the sequences have the same length as the maximum length of the sequences
6. Create the mask for the padded data
7. Convert the input IDs and attention mask into tensors

For more information about the function, my best recommendation would be the post that inspired the creation of this function during the competition: `https://jalammar.github.io/a-visual-guide-to-using-bert-for-the-first-time/`.

After reading the files, we can now move on to processing the data and generating the features:

```
xtrain = pd.read_csv(data_dir + 'train.csv')
xtest = pd.read_csv(data_dir + 'test.csv')
```

We begin by counting the words in the three input components (title, body, and answer) – a simple yet very useful and frequently used feature:

```
for colname in ['question_title', 'question_body', 'answer']:
    newname = colname + '_word_len'

    xtrain[newname] = xtrain[colname].str.split().str.len()
    xtest[newname] = xtest[colname].str.split().str.len()

del newname, colname
```

Exercise 3

Can you think of a way to speed up the preceding code?

Exercise Notes (write down any notes or workings that will help you):

Another useful feature is lexical diversity: a measure of the richness of the vocabulary used in a piece of text. It is typically calculated as the number of unique words in a text divided by the total number of words in it. While it is not directly related to text classification in NLP, it can be a very important factor in certain situations. As an example, if a text contains only a very limited vocabulary, it may be difficult to classify sentiment or predict the characteristics assigned by human evaluators. A good classification model should be able to handle input with a wide range of lexical diversity, but in certain cases high lexical diversity may be beneficial:

```
colname = 'answer'
xtrain[colname+'_div'] = xtrain[colname].apply(lambda s: len(set(s.
split()))) / len(s.split()) )
xtest[colname+'_div'] = xtest[colname].apply(lambda s: len(set(s.split())))
/ len(s.split()) )
```

It is possible to extract many other forms of features purely from descriptive statistics, and since most of them are quite self-explanatory, we present them with minimal comment:

```
## domain components
for df in [xtrain, xtest]:

    df['domcom'] = df['question_user_page'].apply(lambda s: s.split('://')
[1].split('/')[0].split('.'))
    # count components
    df['dom_cnt'] = df['domcom'].apply(lambda s: len(s))
    # pad the length in case some domains have fewer components in the
name
    df['domcom'] = df['domcom'].apply(lambda s: s + ['none', 'none'])

    # components
    for ii in range(0,4):
        df['dom_'+str(ii)] = df['domcom'].apply(lambda s: s[ii])

# clean up
xtrain.drop('domcom', axis = 1, inplace = True)
xtest.drop('domcom', axis = 1, inplace = True)

# shared elements: how many words do the question and answer share?
for df in [xtrain, xtest]:
```

```python
    df['q_words'] = df['question_body'].apply(lambda s: [f for f in
s.split() if f not in eng_stopwords] )
    df['a_words'] = df['answer'].apply(lambda s: [f for f in s.split() if
f not in eng_stopwords] )
    df['qa_word_overlap'] = df.apply(lambda s: len(np.intersect1d(s['q_
words'], s['a_words']))), axis = 1)
    df['qa_word_overlap_norm1'] = df.apply(lambda s: s['qa_word_overlap']/
(1 + len(s['a_words']))), axis = 1)
    df['qa_word_overlap_norm2'] = df.apply(lambda s: s['qa_word_overlap']/
(1 + len(s['q_words']))), axis = 1)
    df.drop(['q_words', 'a_words'], axis = 1, inplace = True)


for df in [xtrain, xtest]:

    ## Number of characters in the text ##
    df["question_title_num_chars"] = df["question_title"].apply(lambda x:
len(str(x)))
    df["question_body_num_chars"] = df["question_body"].apply(lambda x:
len(str(x)))
    df["answer_num_chars"] = df["answer"].apply(lambda x: len(str(x)))


    ## Number of stopwords in the text ##
    df["question_title_num_stopwords"] = df["question_title"].apply(lambda
x: len([w for w in str(x).lower().split() if w in eng_stopwords]))
    df["question_body_num_stopwords"] = df["question_body"].apply(lambda
x: len([w for w in str(x).lower().split() if w in eng_stopwords]))
    df["answer_num_stopwords"] = df["answer"].apply(lambda x: len([w for w
in str(x).lower().split() if w in eng_stopwords]))


    ## Number of punctuations in the text ##
    df["question_title_num_punctuations"] =df['question_title'].
apply(lambda x: len([c for c in str(x) if c in string.punctuation]) )
    df["question_body_num_punctuations"] =df['question_body'].apply(lambda
x: len([c for c in str(x) if c in string.punctuation]) )
    df["answer_num_punctuations"] =df['answer'].apply(lambda x: len([c for
c in str(x) if c in string.punctuation]) )


    ## Number of title case words in the text ##
```

```
    df["question_title_num_words_upper"] = df["question_title"].
apply(lambda x: len([w for w in str(x).split() if w.isupper()]))
    df["question_body_num_words_upper"] = df["question_body"].apply(lambda
x: len([w for w in str(x).split() if w.isupper()]))
    df["answer_num_words_upper"] = df["answer"].apply(lambda x: len([w for
w in str(x).split() if w.isupper()]))
```

For a complete list of the features extracted in this manner, refer to the accompanying notebook in the book's repository: `https://github.com/PacktPublishing/The-Kaggle-Workbook`.

We now proceed with creating another group of features, based on distances between the input components in the embedding space. A fast way of creating quality embeddings for chunks of text is to use a sentence encoder.

Universal Sentence Encoder (USE) is a machine learning model developed by Google that maps natural language sentences into a high-dimensional space, where semantically similar sentences are close to each other. It is trained on a large dataset of diverse natural language text and can be used for various NLP tasks, such as document classification, language translation, and information retrieval.

USE is a type of encoder-decoder model that uses attention mechanisms to encode a variable-length input sequence into a fixed-length vector representation, which is then decoded back into a variable-length output sequence. The encoder processes the input sentence and creates a representation of its meaning, which is then used by the decoder to generate the output sequence.

USE is trained to map a wide range of natural language sentences into a compact and meaningful vector representation, and it is designed to be able to handle a diverse range of languages and sentence structures. It can be used in a variety of applications, including language translation, text classification, and information retrieval. For more information about USE, check out the official project page at `https://tfhub.dev/google/universal-sentence-encoder-large/5`:

```
module_url = "../input/universalsentenceencoderlarge4/"
embed = hub.load(module_url)

embeddings_train = {}
embeddings_test = {}
for text in ['question_title', 'question_body', 'answer']:
    train_text = xtrain[text].str.replace('?', '.').str.replace('!', '.').
tolist()
```

```
        test_text = xtest[text].str.replace('?', '.').str.replace('!', '.').
    tolist()

        curr_train_emb = []
        curr_test_emb = []
        batch_size = 4
        ind = 0
        while ind*batch_size < len(train_text):
            curr_train_emb.append(embed(train_text[ind*batch_size: (ind +
    1)*batch_size])["outputs"].numpy())
            ind += 1

        ind = 0
        while ind*batch_size < len(test_text):
            curr_test_emb.append(embed(test_text[ind*batch_size: (ind +
    1)*batch_size])["outputs"].numpy())
            ind += 1

        embeddings_train[text + '_embedding'] = np.vstack(curr_train_emb)
        embeddings_test[text + '_embedding'] = np.vstack(curr_test_emb)

        print(text)

    del embed
```

Once we have created the embeddings for the title, question, and answer components, we can calculate the distances between them in the embedding space:

```
l2_dist = lambda x, y: np.power(x - y, 2).sum(axis=1)

cos_dist = lambda x, y: (x*y).sum(axis=1)

dist_features_train = np.array([
    l2_dist(embeddings_train['question_title_embedding'], embeddings_
train['answer_embedding']),
    l2_dist(embeddings_train['question_body_embedding'], embeddings_
train['answer_embedding']),
    l2_dist(embeddings_train['question_body_embedding'], embeddings_
train['question_title_embedding']),
```

```
        cos_dist(embeddings_train['question_title_embedding'], embeddings_
    train['answer_embedding']),
        cos_dist(embeddings_train['question_body_embedding'], embeddings_
    train['answer_embedding']),
        cos_dist(embeddings_train['question_body_embedding'], embeddings_
    train['question_title_embedding'])
    ]).T

    dist_features_test = np.array([
        l2_dist(embeddings_test['question_title_embedding'], embeddings_
    test['answer_embedding']),
        l2_dist(embeddings_test['question_body_embedding'], embeddings_
    test['answer_embedding']),
        l2_dist(embeddings_test['question_body_embedding'], embeddings_
    test['question_title_embedding']),
        cos_dist(embeddings_test['question_title_embedding'], embeddings_
    test['answer_embedding']),
        cos_dist(embeddings_test['question_body_embedding'], embeddings_
    test['answer_embedding']),
        cos_dist(embeddings_test['question_body_embedding'], embeddings_
    test['question_title_embedding'])
    ]).T

    del embeddings_train, embeddings_test

    for ii in range(0,6):
        xtrain['dist'+str(ii)] = dist_features_train[:,ii]
        xtest['dist'+str(ii)] = dist_features_test[:,ii]
```

Exercise 4

Examine ways of speeding up the preceding code. Hint: list comprehension.

Also, what are other distance metrics that can be calculated between the vector pairs in the preceding code?

Exercise Notes (write down any notes or workings that will help you):

Having completed the feature preparation part, we can move on to constructing our modeling pipeline. In scikit-learn, pipelines are used to sequentially apply a list of operations to objects that implement fit and transform member functions. This is very useful for composing multiple steps into a single scikit-learn estimator, so that you can train a model with multiple steps in a single call instead of having to train each step separately. We will utilize this approach to preprocess the text data, extract features, and estimate a predictive model.

An important component of our feature extraction pipeline is the TfidfVectorizer: **Term Frequency-Inverse Document Frequency (TF-IDF)** is a method for vectorizing text data that is commonly used in NLP. The TF-IDF vectorizer works by tokenizing the input text into individual words (or sub-words) and then calculating the score – a product of **Term Frequency (TF)** measuring the number of times a word appears in the document, and the **Inverse Document Frequency (IDF)** measuring the rarity of the word across the corpus. Combining those for each word in the text, we can create a vector representation of the text that can subsequently be used as input to a machine learning model. Below, we define numerous pipelines for different fields from the (title, question, and answer) set – focusing purely on the handling of the textual representation of the input.

We begin by creating two transformations of the title field: one on the word level and the other on the character level. To control the size of the resulting vectors, we limit the former to 25,000 features and the latter to 5,000. The max_features parameter means that the TfidfVectorizer will only consider the top max_features most frequent words/characters when creating the TF-IDF matrix described previously:

```
limit_word = 25000
limit_char = 5000

title_col = 'question_title'
title_transformer = Pipeline([
    ('tfidf', TfidfVectorizer(lowercase = False,
max_df = 0.3, min_df = 1,
binary = False, use_idf = True,
smooth_idf = False,
            ngram_range = (1,2), stop_words = 'english',
            token_pattern = '(?u)\\b\\w+\\b' ,
max_features = limit_word ))
])
```

```
title_transformer2 = Pipeline([
    ('tfidf2',  TfidfVectorizer( sublinear_tf=True,
    strip_accents='unicode', analyzer='char',
    stop_words='english', ngram_range=(1, 4),
max_features= limit_char))
])


body_col = 'question_body'
body_transformer = Pipeline([
    ('tfidf',TfidfVectorizer(lowercase = False, max_df = 0.3, min_df = 1,
                             binary = False, use_idf = True, smooth_idf =
False,
                             ngram_range = (1,2), stop_words = 'english',
                             token_pattern = '(?u)\\b\\w+\\b' , max_
features = limit_word ))
])


body_transformer2 = Pipeline([
    ('tfidf2',  TfidfVectorizer( sublinear_tf=True,
    strip_accents='unicode', analyzer='char',
    stop_words='english', ngram_range=(1, 4), max_features= limit_char))
])


answer_col = 'answer'

answer_transformer = Pipeline([
    ('tfidf', TfidfVectorizer(lowercase = False, max_df = 0.3, min_df = 1,
                              binary = False, use_idf = True, smooth_idf =
False,
                              ngram_range = (1,2), stop_words = 'english',
                              token_pattern = '(?u)\\b\\w+\\b' , max_
features = limit_word ))
])


answer_transformer2 = Pipeline([
    ('tfidf2',  TfidfVectorizer( sublinear_tf=True,
```

```
        strip_accents='unicode', analyzer='char',
        stop_words='english', ngram_range=(1, 4), max_features= limit_char))
])
```

Exercise 5

Investigate the impact different arguments for TfidfVectorizer can have on the model performance.

Exercise Notes (write down any notes or workings that will help you):

Our feature space contains multiple numerical features – descriptive statistics, as well as distances between embeddings – that we created earlier, and those need to be processed, for obvious reasons, in a slightly different manner than the text fields:

```
num_cols = [
    'question_title_word_len', 'question_body_word_len', 'answer_
word_len','answer_div','question_title_num_chars','question_body_num_
chars','answer_num_chars',  'question_title_num_stopwords','question_body_
num_stopwords','answer_num_stopwords',
    'question_title_num_punctuations','question_body_num_
punctuations','answer_num_punctuations''question_title_num_words_
upper','question_body_num_words_upper','answer_num_words_upper',
    'dist0', 'dist1', 'dist2', 'dist3', 'dist4', 'dist5'
]
```

We apply light processing to the numerical columns:

- SimpleImputer is a scikit-learn class for imputing missing values in a dataset. It provides basic strategies for imputing missing values, such as using a constant or the mean or median value.

- PowerTransformer performs a power transform on the data, which serves the purpose of stabilizing variance and moving the data distribution closer to Gaussianity (helpful if we want to apply a linear model to those features).

```
num_transformer = Pipeline([
    ('impute', SimpleImputer(strategy='constant', fill_value=0)),
    ('scale', PowerTransformer(method='yeo-johnson'))
])
```

Finally, we have the categorical columns created previously:

```
cat_cols = [
    'dom_0', 'dom_1', 'dom_2',
    'dom_3', 'category',
    'is_question_no_name_user',
    'is_answer_no_name_user',
    'dom_cnt'
]

cat_transformer = Pipeline([
```

```
    ('impute', SimpleImputer(strategy='constant', fill_value='')),
    ('encode', OneHotEncoder(handle_unknown='ignore'))
])
```

We can combine all the elements above into a single transformer that processes the entire content of our feature space:

```
preprocessor = ColumnTransformer(
    transformers = [
        ('title', title_transformer, title_col),
        ('title2', title_transformer2, title_col),
        ('body', body_transformer, body_col),
        ('body2', body_transformer2, body_col),
        ('answer', answer_transformer, answer_col),
        ('answer2', answer_transformer2, answer_col),
        ('num', num_transformer, num_cols),
        ('cat', cat_transformer, cat_cols)
    ]
)
```

Finally, we need an actual regression model to make use of all those features. Since this is a simple baseline, we go for ridge regression: as a reminder, it's a linear regression model that uses L2 regularization to improve the generalization of the model and prevent overfitting. L2 regularization adds a penalty term to the loss function of the model, which is proportional to the sum of squared weights. As a result, the model is "encouraged" to use smaller weights, which can also improve the interpretability:

```
pipeline = Pipeline([
    ('preprocessor', preprocessor),
    ('estimator',Ridge(random_state=RANDOM_STATE))
])
```

Exercise 6

What possibilities, other than ridge, do we have for regularizing a linear model?

Exercise Notes (write down any notes or workings that will help you):

We go through the basic preparation for fitting the model, like separating the ID column or the targets:

```
# preparation
id_train = xtrain['qa_id']
ytrain = xtrain[target_cols]
xtrain.drop(target_cols + ['qa_id'], axis = 1, inplace = True)

id_test = xtest['qa_id']
xtest.drop('qa_id', axis = 1, inplace = True)

dropcols = ['question_user_name', 'question_user_page',
 'answer_user_name', 'answer_user_page','url','host']

xtrain.drop(dropcols, axis = 1, inplace = True)
xtest.drop(dropcols, axis = 1, inplace = True)
```

We will evaluate the performance of our baseline model using **Out-of-Fold (OOF)** cross-validation. OOF is a method used to evaluate the performance of a machine learning model by training the model on a portion of the available data and evaluating it on the remaining portion. It is a way to obtain an estimate of the model's generalization performance, which is how well the model will perform on new, unseen data.

OOF cross-validation involves dividing the available data into a number of folds, typically 5 or 10, and training the model on a different subset of the data each time, leaving one fold as the validation set and using the other folds for training. This process is repeated until each fold has been used as the validation set once, and the average performance across all the folds is taken as the OOF performance.

Splitting the data into folds can be done in multiple ways – in this instance we need to take into account the fact that questions are not unique, i.e., multiple records can correspond to the same question with different answers (and hence be evaluated differently by the human evaluators). This means we need to make sure each question appears in one fold only – and for that end we use GroupKFold. This manner of computing validation folds is a variation of k-fold cross-validation, used when the data is divided into groups (for example, when each sample belongs to a certain class):

```
nfolds = 5
mvalid = np.zeros((xtrain.shape[0], len(target_cols)))
```

```
mfull = np.zeros((xtest.shape[0], len(target_cols)))

kf = GroupKFold(n_splits= nfolds).split(X=xtrain.question_body,
groups=xtrain.question_body)
```

This code first splits the data into five folds using the KFold class from scikit-learn, then iterates through each step (from 1 to nfolds), splitting the data into training and validation sets and fitting the model on the training data. The model is then evaluated on the validation data and the score is added to the list of scores. Finally, the mean score across all the folds is calculated and stored in the mean_score variable. This mean score can be used as an estimate of the model's OOF performance.

We follow with a standard procedure for computing OOF model performance:

1. For each fold, generate the training/validation sets
2. Estimate a ridge regression model for each of the target columns in this split
3. Store the predictions
4. Save the model in a pickle file for reuse later on

A few words are in order for this last point: the pickle format is a common way to serialize objects in Python and is a perfectly reasonable way of making your iterative workflow faster (so you don't have to refit the pipeline every time). The moment you start using pickle in a collaborative environment, there are two aspects that need to be taken into account:

*   Pickle is not human-readable, and it is not guaranteed to be backward-compatible between different versions of Python or the libraries used to create the pickled objects
*   The pickle format is vulnerable to malicious attacks, as a maliciously crafted pickle could contain arbitrary code that is executed when the file is unpickled

The following code chunk demonstrates how to calculate the model performance on out-of-fold predictions:

*   For each fold, we split the data into training and test datasets: the former is used to fit the model, the latter for performance evaluation
*   We fit a separate pipeline (preprocessing + ridge regression model) for each column
*   The trained model for this fold is saved into an appropriate pickle file

- The predictions are stored in the mvalid/mfull arrays for later use in computing the score and preparing a submission, respectively.

```
for ind, (train_index, test_index) in enumerate(kf):

    # split
    x0, x1 = xtrain.loc[train_index], xtrain.loc[test_index]
    y0, y1 = ytrain.loc[train_index], ytrain.loc[test_index]

    for ii in range(0, ytrain.shape[1]):

        # fit model
        be = clone(pipeline)
        be.fit(x0, np.array(y0)[:,ii])

        filename = 'ridge_f' + str(ind) + '_c' + str(ii) + '.pkl'
        pickle.dump(be, open(filename, 'wb'))

        # park forecast
        mvalid[test_index, ii] = be.predict(x1)
        mfull[:,ii] += be.predict(xtest)/nfolds

    print('---')
```

We can evaluate the performance of our model by computing the Spearman correlation (our competition metric) for each column of the OOF predictions and then averaging across all columns:

```
corvec = np.zeros((ytrain.shape[1],1))
for ii in range(0, ytrain.shape[1]):
    mvalid[:,ii] = rankdata(mvalid[:,ii])/mvalid.shape[0]
    mfull[:,ii] = rankdata(mfull[:,ii])/mfull.shape[0]

    corvec[ii] = stats.spearmanr(ytrain[ytrain.columns[ii]], mvalid[:,ii])
[0]

print(corvec.mean())
0.3041
```

The obtained result for the competition metric is 0.3041.

Exercise 7

How does the model performance change for a different number of folds? Examine using a low number of folds (for example, 3) and a high number (for example, 10).

Exercise Notes (write down any notes or workings that will help you):

In this section, we have demonstrated how to build a baseline solution using relatively simple methods: descriptive statistics on the text fields, combined with embedding from a pretrained model, not tuned to the task at hand. While not sufficient to reach a medal zone, this approach serves as a useful foundation for the next section: analyzing the top solutions and the insights they give about our problem.

Learning from top solutions

The baseline approach described above is a good starting point – but how did it perform in the competition itself? Quite well, as it turns out: Chris Deotte (`https://www.kaggle.com/cdeotte`) started with the meta-features and, by fitting an intermediate LightGBM model, was able to discover some interesting relationships that informed his next steps in the model-building process: `https://www.kaggle.com/competitions/google-quest-challenge/discussion/130041`.

A second interesting insight from the solution proposed by Chris (which scored one spot below the silver medal zone in the private leaderboard) was post-processing: by extensive cross-validation, he determined the appropriate ranges for clipping predictions for different columns. This strategy improved the competition metric considerably:

```
clippings = {
    'question_has_commonly_accepted_answer':[0,0.6],
    'question_conversational':[0.15,1],
    'question_multi_intent':[0.1,1],
    'question_type_choice':[0.1,1],
    'question_type_compare':[0.1,1],
    'question_type_consequence':[0.08,1],
    'question_type_definition':[0.1,1],
    'question_type_entity':[0.13,1]
}
```

All the high-performing solutions in this competition involved training a BERT-type model; an excellent notebook for those exploring the approach is the solution posted by akensert (`https://www.kaggle.com/akensert`), where he demonstrated how to build a complete BERT pipeline from scratch in TensorFlow: `https://www.kaggle.com/code/akensert/quest-bert-base-tf2-0?scriptVersionId=39570432`.

Finally, we close this section with an absolute must-read: an interview with the winning team "bibimorph" composed of Dmytro Danevskyi (`https://www.kaggle.com/ddanevskyi`), Yury Kashnitsky (`https://www.kaggle.com/kashnitsky`), Oleg Yaroshevskiy (`https://www.kaggle.com/yaroshevskiy`), and Dmitry Abulkhanov (`https://www.kaggle.com/dmitriyab`). The interview was published on Medium at `https://medium.com/kaggle-blog/the-3-ingredients-to-our-success-winners-dish-on-their-solution-to-googles-quest-q-a-labeling-c1a63014b88`, and it is definitely worth studying in detail.

Let's summarize the most important points and findings shared by the winners. First, the language model pretraining:

- Transfer learning was key to the team performance; the small dataset available in the competition meant that leveraging unlabeled data was of paramount importance.
- Specifically, the team used a Stack Overflow corpus to fine-tune a BERT model through the **Masked Language Model (MLM)** task. You can find out more about MLM in the BERT paper: `https://arxiv.org/abs/1810.04805`.
- They added auxiliary targets, which they engineered specifically on the external corpus.
- The combination of transfer learning and domain adaptation was instrumental in their success.

The next important component was the pseudo-labeling, which followed these steps:

1. Train the model with labeled data
2. Predict the labels for unlabeled data – those predictions are referred to as pseudo-labels
3. Retrain the model using all the available data and combine the original with the pseudo-labels

Exercise 8

Investigate pseudo-labeling and think of a case when it might not work, i.e., as a result of applying pseudo-labeling, the performance might deteriorate.

Exercise Notes (write down any notes or workings that will help you):

Finally, post-process the predictions. The competition metric (the Spearman correlation) is defined in terms of ranks; as such, it is sensitive to the observations being equal (ties present in the sample). The team worked around this problem by bucketing the predictions from their model in a manner that mimicked the distribution of the data:

```python
# Applying postprocessing to the final blend
def postprocess_single(target, ref):
    """

    The idea here is to make the distribution of a particular predicted
    column to match the corresponding distribution of the corresponding column
    in the training dataset (called ref here)
    """

    ids = np.argsort(target)
    counts = sorted(Counter(ref).items(), key=lambda s: s[0])
    scores = np.zeros_like(target)

    last_pos = 0
    v = 0

    for value, count in counts:
        next_pos = last_pos + int(round(count / len(ref) * len(target)))
        if next_pos == last_pos:
            next_pos += 1

        cond = ids[last_pos:next_pos]
        scores[cond] = v
        last_pos = next_pos
        v += 1

    return scores / scores.max()
```

The preceding function is taken from the GitHub repository of one of the participants: https://github.com/oleg-yaroshevskiy/quest_qa_labeling/blob/yorko/step11_final/blending_n_postprocessing.py#L48:

1. It begins by sorting the target column by its index and creating a list of counts of the unique values, sorted by the values themselves

2. The function iterates through the counts list, and for each count, it calculates the next position in the target that should be modified

3. It subsequently assigns the current value to the slice of the target column and increments the value along with the last modified position

4. The resulting array is normalized to have a maximum value of 1

Reading the interview and following the provided links equips you with the knowledge necessary to go through the actual solution with code; here is the post summarizing the winning solution in the competition forum: https://www.kaggle.com/competitions/google-quest-challenge/discussion/129840.

The basic pipeline can be found at https://www.kaggle.com/code/phoenix9032/pytorch-bert-plain/notebook.

One notable element is the structured approach to experimentation: defining a class for pipeline configuration:

```
class PipeLineConfig:
    def __init__(self, lr, warmup,accum_steps, epochs, seed, expname,head_
tail,freeze,question_weight,answer_weight,fold,train):
        self.lr = lr
        self.warmup = warmup
        self.accum_steps = accum_steps
        self.epochs = epochs
        self.seed = seed
        self.expname = expname
        self.head_tail = head_tail
        self.freeze = freeze
        self.question_weight = question_weight
        self.answer_weight =answer_weight
        self.fold = fold
        self.train = train
```

Once defined, we can ensure experiment reproducibility, as well as quick iterations between different models.

Exercise 9

Use the notebook linked above as a basis for your own solution. Run it block by block, checking that you understand the underlying mechanics.

Exercise Notes (write down any notes or workings that will help you):

Summary

In this chapter, we have examined an approach to NLP competitions, specifically Google Quest Q&A Labeling. We began with a baseline utilizing vintage methods (summary/descriptive characteristics of the text fields), combined with embeddings from a pretrained model. This gave us a foundational understanding of the challenges involved, and we then moved on to a discussion of more advanced solutions that performed well in the competition. This chapter should give you an understanding of how to approach NLP classification contests; those new to the field will benefit from the baseline solution, while more experienced Kagglers can benefit from the guidance that the published medal approaches provide.

Join our book's Discord space

Join our Discord community to meet like-minded people and learn alongside more than 2000 members at:

`https://packt.link/KaggleDiscord`

packt.com

Subscribe to our online digital library for full access to over 7,000 books and videos, as well as industry leading tools to help you plan your personal development and advance your career. For more information, please visit our website.

Why subscribe?

- Spend less time learning and more time coding with practical eBooks and Videos from over 4,000 industry professionals
- Improve your learning with Skill Plans built especially for you
- Get a free eBook or video every month
- Fully searchable for easy access to vital information
- Copy and paste, print, and bookmark content

At www.packt.com, you can also read a collection of free technical articles, sign up for a range of free newsletters, and receive exclusive discounts and offers on Packt books and eBooks.

Other Books You May Enjoy

If you enjoyed this book, you may be interested in these other books by Packt:

The Kaggle Book

Konrad Banachewicz

Luca Massaron

ISBN: 978-1-80181-747-9

- Get acquainted with Kaggle as a competition platform
- Make the most of Kaggle Notebooks, Datasets, and Discussion forums
- Create a portfolio of projects and ideas to get further in your career
- Design k-fold and probabilistic validation schemes
- Get to grips with common and never-before-seen evaluation metrics
- Understand binary and multi-class classification and object detection
- Approach NLP and time series tasks more effectively
- Handle simulation and optimization competitions on Kaggle

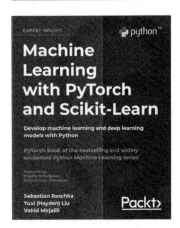

Machine Learning with PyTorch and Scikit-Learn

Sebastian Raschka

Yuxi (Hayden) Liu

ISBN: 978-1-80181-931-2

- Explore frameworks, models, and techniques for machines to 'learn' from data
- Use scikit-learn for machine learning and PyTorch for deep learning
- Train machine learning classifiers on images, text, and more
- Build and train neural networks, transformers, and boosting algorithms
- Discover best practices for evaluating and tuning models
- Predict continuous target outcomes using regression analysis
- Dig deeper into textual and social media data using sentiment analysis

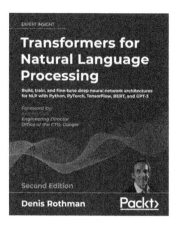

Transformers for Natural Language Processing – Second Edition

Denis Rothman

ISBN: 978-1-80324-733-5

- Find out how ViT and CLIP label images (including blurry ones!) and create images from a sentence using DALL-E
- Discover new techniques to investigate complex language problems
- Compare and contrast the results of GPT-3 against T5, GPT-2, and BERT-based transformers
- Carry out sentiment analysis, text summarization, casual speech analysis, machine translations, and more using TensorFlow, PyTorch, and GPT-3
- Measure the productivity of key transformers to define their scope, potential, and limits in production

Packt is searching for authors like you

If you're interested in becoming an author for Packt, please visit `authors.packtpub.com` and apply today. We have worked with thousands of developers and tech professionals, just like you, to help them share their insight with the global tech community. You can make a general application, apply for a specific hot topic that we are recruiting an author for, or submit your own idea.

Share your thoughts

Now you've finished *The Kaggle Workbook*, we'd love to hear your thoughts! Scan the QR code below to go straight to the Amazon review page for this book and share your feedback or leave a review on the site that you purchased it from.

`https://packt.link/r/1-804-61121-2`

Your review is important to us and the tech community and will help us make sure we're delivering excellent quality content.

Index

Download a free PDF copy of this book

Thanks for purchasing this book!

Do you like to read on the go but are unable to carry your print books everywhere? Is your eBook purchase not compatible with the device of your choice?

Don't worry, now with every Packt book you get a DRM-free PDF version of that book at no cost.

Read anywhere, any place, on any device. Search, copy, and paste code from your favorite technical books directly into your application.

The perks don't stop there, you can get exclusive access to discounts, newsletters, and great free content in your inbox daily

Follow these simple steps to get the benefits:

1. Scan the QR code or visit the link below

https://packt.link/free-ebook/9781804611210

2. Submit your proof of purchase
3. That's it! We'll send your free PDF and other benefits to your email directly

Printed in Great Britain
by Amazon

29045096R00097